Green Ut

GREEN UTOPIAS

Environmental Hope Before and After Nature

Lisa Garforth

polity

The right of Lisa Garforth to be identified as Author of this Work has been asserted in accordance with the UK Copyright, Designs and Patents Act 1988.

First published in 2018 by Polity Press

Polity Press
65 Bridge Street
Cambridge CB2 1UR, UK

Polity Press
101 Station Landing, Suite 300
Medford, MA 02155, USA

ISBN-13: 978-0-7456-8473-4
ISBN-13: 978-0-7456-8474-1(pb)

A catalogue record for this book is available from the British Library.

Typeset in 10.5 on 12 pt Sabon
by Toppan Best-set Premedia Limited
Printed and bound in Great Britain by CPI Group (UK) Ltd, Croydon

The publisher has used its best endeavours to ensure that the URLs for external websites referred to in this book are correct and active at the time of going to press. However, the publisher has no responsibility for the websites and can make no guarantee that a site will remain live or that the content is or will remain appropriate.

Every effort has been made to trace all copyright holders, but if any have been inadvertently overlooked the publisher will be pleased to include any necessary credits in any subsequent reprint or edition.

For further information on Polity, visit our website:
politybooks.com

Contents

Acknowledgements

This book draws together research and writing from more than fifteen years of thinking about environmental utopianism. Over that time I have benefitted from the wisdom and ideas of many people. I want to especially mention Andy Tudor, Ruth Levitas, Steve Yearley for their early support, and Tom Moylan and Peter Phillimore for wise comments on the draft manuscript. For invaluable help along the way I thank Lena Eriksson, Shona Hunter and Christopher Barber.

1

Introduction: Utopia, Environment and Nature

Other green worlds

Every day seems to bring more news of environmental disaster. Flooded streets don't just bring chaos and loss to those who live there. Their images resonate through media networks with the threat of widespread climate change effects. The news media explodes around the latest scientific statement on global warming and then turns away, creating a silence or indifference in which it seems impossible that anything can be done. Hollywood films rehearse spectacular environmental disasters which only a lucky (or unlucky) few will survive, or present grim, grey worlds of endemic environmental dysfunction. Booker prize-winning novelists write trilogies tracing the collapse of biodiversity and the rise of genetically engineered posthumans. Young adult fiction offers dystopias set on the rising waters of a warming world. A wildlife documentary presenter looks at us through the tv screen; he gestures at the blank white icescape behind him and tells us that it is irreversibly melting. We wince then turn off the television, put out our recycling, get on with the next thing.

In the midst of these pessimistic, dystopian and apocalyptic narratives, it can seem that there are few hopeful images of or statements about greener futures in our culture. The environmental campaigner Jonathan Porritt (2011) has expressed concern that a lack of positive visions makes it hard to imagine what sustainability might mean. But in fact all sorts of hopes and desires for better socio-environmental futures are at work across contemporary Western philosophy, politics and literature. Since the 1960s, environmentalism has warned about the dire consequences of abusing and exploiting the planet's natural resources, imagining future wastelands of ecological depletion and social chaos. But it has also generated rich new ideas about how humans might live better with nature. Environmentalists have warned that natural resources may run out, but they have also tried to show how we might live happier and more fulfilling lives by consuming less and making our relationships more fulfilling. Ecological philosophers have criticized modernity's dominant technocentrism and its instrumental attitude towards nature, but they have also explored the pleasures that valuing nature for its own sake might bring. Speculative fictions envisage post-apocalyptic wastelands, but also moments of joy and hope, and even descriptions of life in sustainable society.

Sometimes these green hopes take the form of a clear, detailed and explicit blueprint for the future: a manifesto or an explicitly utopian novel. But desires for a greener future can also be more obscure, fragmented and fleeting. Sometimes green alternatives are framed in terms of a coherent set of ecological values or politics. Sometimes they speak more loosely to a desire to protect or love or 'get back' to nature. The content, the form, the values of this green utopianism are diverse – they express different hopes in different ways. They vary over time and between societies and social groups. But they are more common than we might initially imagine.

This book, then, is about green utopianism. It explores some of the ways in which Western cultures have imagined better futures for human societies with nature since the emergence of the idea of environmental crisis in the 1960s and 1970s. This was a time when public talk about the future of nature was dominated by ideas of imminent ends (of resources), physical limits (to growth), and looming catastrophe (environmental and social). Closely linked to this crisis sensibility was a powerful sense that things could be different, that we could build societies in tune with nature that would be more sustainable, more satisfying and more secure.

In some ways those hopes have become familiar and mainstream. In other ways those futures seem more unattainable and more idealistic than ever in the face of grim climate predictions and arguments that we face the end of nature. So as well as the hopeful ideas that suffused early environmentalism, this book explores the kinds of green visions that are currently available in our culture. Green hope is more widespread, I argue, but at the same time less visionary and radical. Desires for a better greener future are still there, but they are less explicit and powerful, more fugitive and fleeting, often framed by narratives of loss and mourning.

Although the idea of utopia often gets a bad press, in this book I claim it unashamedly as an invaluable way of exploring images of and desires for a better way of living (Levitas 2010 [1990]: 9). Utopianism is about dreams and hopes for an alternative to the social arrangements that we currently have. Utopian thinking runs through art and politics, public debate and popular culture. I argue that it is critically important as we look forward to the possibility of a different environmental future and learn to take responsibility for what modern humans have done with and to nature in the past. Sometimes utopias are born of passionate and heartfelt political commitments, individual or collective. Sometimes the hope for a better world seems to happen despite conscious individual intentions (Garforth 2009). Either way, utopias are vital cultural spaces in which the taken-for-granted arrangements and practices of our everyday lives can be made strange, in which we can reflect critically on the big picture of what is happening in our social world, and through which we can explore alternatives. But it is not an unproblematic kind of thinking, so I also use the word utopia with some care. For many utopia is associated with rigid blueprints of perfection, totalitarian master plans or fantastical idealism. In what follows I will draw on less negative and more nuanced definitions to show how utopia should be understood as a social and cultural process that is partial and provisional, critical and creative.

If I use the word 'utopia' unabashedly, I use the word 'green' more cautiously. In this book I look back over the short history of Western environmentalist thought and ecological philosophy from the 1960s to the early twenty-first century. As a political, social and philosophical movement, environmentalism has focused on the problematic ways in which Western societies have treated nature. It has produced powerful new ideas about how those societies could instead both protect the planet and enhance human well-being. It has explored ecocentric positions in which nature is held to have intrinsic value separate from human perceptions, needs and uses. But environmentalism has also tended to treat the category of nature as unproblematic, as conceptually separate from society and culture. In contemporary science, philosophy and social theory there are serious challenges to these distinctions and assumptions, and compelling proposals for rearranging our worldly ontologies. Some question the idea that nature is 'One Thing with One Name' (Cronon 1996: 35) and critique environmentalist attempts to defend non-human nature primarily on the basis of its separation from human societies. Some argue that we can imagine an 'ecology without nature' (Morton 2007); some celebrate nature's end as the beginning of a new kind of ecological politics (Latour 2004). I use the word 'green', then, to suggest the complicated, dissonant bodies of thought that take part in ongoing contestations and debate about political and cultural ideas of the environment, rather than working with a strict or narrow definition of deep ecology or environmentalism.

I also argue that as arguments about the end of nature and the beginning of the Anthropocene circulate around Western cultures, the conditions for green utopianism have changed significantly. Where once environmental debates focused on the prospects for continuity and recuperation – sustainable development, ecological caution and protecting nature – now the dominant problematic is how we are to learn to live in a fundamentally different and unpredictable era. In what follows I take this transition seriously and try to trace green utopias before and after nature. The Anthropocene refers to a new geological era in which human activities are the dominant influence on the natural environment. It is also a cultural era in which we constantly reflect upon this state of affairs. The end-of-nature proposals that I discuss here are part of debates about what anthropogenic climate change means to and for us – materially, conceptually, politically, affectively – and how it changes our sense of the histories and futures we are making and have made. As I have noted above, the idea of a separate nature has been crucial to ecological political philosophy as well as to modern Western science and culture. Once we start to think about the mixed-up, hybrid worlds that we have made and that we must live in and with (Latour 2004), and about the complex ways in which we ourselves are simultaneously matter and culture (Haraway 1991; Bennett 2010), we need new ontologies, new ethics and new ways of thinking about better greener worlds.

So in this book I trace a shift from utopias of sustainability to postnatural visions and try to locate the prospects for green hope when there is no separate nature in which to root it – and arguably a limited sense of the future in which green alternatives might unfold. I focus on a relatively limited body of utopian thinking and ideas: environmentalism, ecological political philosophy, and speculative fiction. This is not to deny the existence or value of a much broader field of green utopianism. Below I will sketch an argument about the ubiquity and formal diversity of utopian desires and expressions. A broad and inclusive definition of utopianism would include: ideas about better greener futures informing innovative technologies from genetic modification to the internet of things to zero-emission buildings; ecotopian experiments from ecovillages to smart cities to re-wilding urban spaces; movements such as slow food, permaculture farming or carbon-rationing groups; activist and local green visions; climate action plans. I have focused primarily, however, on discourses and representations relating to better greener worlds as they have emerged in mainstream environmentalism, well-established ecophilosophy and theory, and in self-consciously environmentalist fiction.

Other reviews and analyses have explored utopias beyond concepts and texts and examined how utopia is performed and enacted individually and collectively at a variety of scales and in multiple spaces. Attention to the material, physical, interactional and practised dimensions of green utopianism has been growing in recent years. Studies have looked at intentional communities, including environmental ones (Pepper 1991; Sargisson and Sargent 2004; Sargisson 2007a, 2007b, 2012; Miles 2008; Fremeaux and Jordan 2010; Andreas and Wagner 2012). Analyses of utopias in relation to lifestyle, everyday practice and embedded citizenship are increasingly prominent in the field (Gardiner 2001; Firth 2012; Cooper 2014). Social and political scientists have explored utopian strands of 'transitions to sustainable living' (Leonard and Barry 2009): green urban and community projects including the transition towns movement; green co-housing initiatives; autonomous urbanism and squatting movements; alternative economies; sustainable architecture and planning practices; temporary ecological occupations of public spaces (Kraftl 2006; Miles 2008; Jamison 2010; Pickerill 2010, 2012; Brown et al. 2012; Davies and Leonard 2012; Bradley and Hedrén 2015).

My approach does not capture these important and innovative strands of green utopian thought and practice. But my more selective focus enables me to look closely at some of the most dominant narratives and frameworks for understanding environmental dilemmas and green hopes. This allows a modestly interdisciplinary focus that moves across politics and policy discourses, philosophy and social theory, developments in mainstream environmental ideas and radical ecopolitical thought, speculative literature and literary criticism. It also allows me to pay attention to important changes in major environmental discourses and cultural articulations of green ideas over the last fifty years or so. The successive constellations of green utopian ideas that I have analysed are necessarily indicative and partial rather than exhaustive and systematic. I have not sought to make hard and fast periodizations, but attempted rather to feel out historically situated clusters of concerns and concepts and analyse continuities and differences. Looking across a loosely chronological and overlapping set of ideas reveals something new about the nature of green hopes and the changing contexts in which we articulate and express them in particular periods.

What I offer here, then, is a new reflection on some well-known strands of green thinking over the last fifty years. One way of looking at this is that utopia offers a novel lens through which to understand debates and developments in green political thought in that period. Ecopolitical philosophy frequently touches on the value and relevance of utopian ideals to green political ideologies and political movements (Eckersley 1992; Dobson 1995; Torgerson 1999; Harvey

2000; Pepper 2005). But identifying a wider stream of green utopianism enables us to trace the ebbs and flows of hope and future visions across environmental discourses and situate more radical ecocentric visions in relation to their broader environmentalist context. Adding utopian and speculative fiction to this mix offers to enrich our understanding of green political thought. Fiction does not simply illustrate ecological ethics and ideas. Narrative offers a distinctive approach to exploring alternative green values, translating them into social experiences and ways of life. As Moylan argues, it is not just the content of ecological ideas that matters here. The form is crucial. Science fiction world-building creates new possibilities for estranged speculation, visioning beyond 'the limits of the present' (Moylan 2011: 26). If science fiction is 'our culture's vast, shared polyvocal archive of the possible' (Canavan 2014: 16), examining that archive's traces of ecotopia brings a fresh perspective to green political debates.

The book can also be seen as a synthesis of otherwise disparate approaches to green hope in utopian studies. Previous studies of green utopias have mainly emerged from debates in political science and philosophy and from studies of science fiction. Some have focused on describing and comparing the content of ecological visions across a long history of utopian texts (De Geus 1999). Some, as I note above, have discussed the value of utopian ideas for ecological political ideologies and practical environmental politics. Others have examined the transgressive utopian ideas of radical ecocentric philosophy (Sargisson 2000, 2012). A growing number of studies have focused on speculative fiction (Murphy 2000; Yanarella 2001; more recently, Otto 2012; Canavan and Robinson 2014). These approaches are surprisingly divergent, however, covering different historical periods, texts and genres. I hope to suggest a contextualizing framework within which the connections between them might be understood and to offer a more synthetic approach to the recent history of green utopias than currently exists in the field.

It will be clear even from this brief outline, then, that the concepts of both utopia and nature are rich, contested and shifting. The relationships between them are necessarily various and complex. Even since the 1970s, there have been marked shifts in the green futures that it has been possible to imagine. Continuing threads of green hope can be traced throughout this period, but there have also been reversals, reinventions and renewals. Environmental utopias develop in relation to specific political, social and intellectual contexts. Different green visions emerge in response to new framings of social-natural problems and dilemmas, and from changing experiences of living in and with different kinds of environments. To understand how this works, we need to look more closely at what we understand by utopias and utopianism, and how we can think with them.

Thinking with utopias

Utopias are often dismissed as rigid blueprints linked to totalitarian attempts to impose a new way of life on a nation or people. They are associated, as Jameson remarks sardonically, with 'a will to power over all those individuals for whom you are plotting an ironclad happiness' (2000: 383). For some, the very idea of a perfect society constitutes a denial of fundamental human qualities (fallibility, creativity). Pursuing the vision of an ideal republic amounts to a denial of democracy and the open society (Gray 2008; Popper 2013 [1945]). Here utopia is an attempt to achieve perfection and freeze social life forever in one static arrangement. It is contrasted with the lively, messy reality of politics and social change. For others, utopia is equated with impossible and impractical dreams and fantasies. Here utopia is a grand scheme for human betterment that is too big and too far-fetched to come about, a whimsical pipedream for social improvement or moral enhancement that distracts from practical politics and reform. Popular ideas of utopia, then, are associated with the two equally off-putting poles: totalitarian violence and dreamy ineffectuality. Utopian thinking is also seen, albeit perhaps implicitly, as a minority interest: something for politicians, demagogues, dictators, drop-outs or fantasists, not something that most of us indulge in.

But we can and should understand utopias and utopianism differently. The field of utopian studies that has developed over the last thirty years has generated new definitions and approaches. It has shown how widespread utopianism is, and how utopias might matter for and to everyone. Utopian scholars insist that utopias are not reducible to blueprints or pipedreams. They invite us to think of utopias instead as visions that stimulate critical and creative reflection on alternatives to the way things are. In Levitas's concise and persuasive formulation, utopia is simply 'an expression of desire for a different way of living and being' (2010 [1990]: 9). The inclusive definitions of utopia that now dominate the field of utopian studies emphasize ubiquity (Sargent 1994; Jameson 2005; Levitas 2010 [1990], 2013). Utopias and utopian desires are seen as ordinary and everyday rather than unusual or esoteric (Gardiner 2001; Cooper 2014). As Lefebvre put it, '[w]e are all utopians, so soon as we wish for something different and stop playing the part of the faithful performer or watchdog' (1990 [1971]: 75). Utopia involves, then, a capacity to be critical of present social arrangements and to creatively imagine alternatives, however briefly and superficially. On these grounds we can see it as commonplace. It emerges from everyday experiences of dissatisfaction, in-equality or lack (Bloch 1986; Levitas 2010 [1990]).

Within this broad definition, it is useful to distinguish between utopianism and utopias (Jameson 2005), or similarly between the broad phenomenon of 'social dreaming' and the particular 'faces' through which these dreams are expressed (Sargent 1994: 1). On the one hand we can think about a general capacity and tendency of humans individually and collectively to desire something different and better (utopian-ism, a utopian impulse). On the other, we can identify the particular visions through which these desires are expressed (utopias, utopian programmes). Utopias become objects or things when desires for something different are articulated and elaborated into a detailed vision of a social alternative. But they are part of a wider process of utopianism, acts and moments of desiring something different that are not reducible to any particular utopian plan or vision. Utopia therefore is a processual affair. Engaging with any particular utopian vision is part of a wider process of expressing desires for something different, encountering the possibility of oth-erness, and changing individual consciousness and cultural frameworks.

For some theorists, the propensity to imagine the world otherwise and desire a better way of living is a 'defining, constitutive' aspect of the human psyche (Bauman 2003: 11; see also 2009 [1976]; Bloch 1986; Geoghegan 1987). Others reject the idea of an essential utopian impulse and prefer, like Levitas, to frame the capacity to imagine and explore alternatives as a response to the experience of lack or absence. Utopia is the outcome of needs and wants generated but unfulfilled by a given set of social arrangements (Levitas 2010 [1990]: 9). When we are unhappy, unfulfilled or alienated, we imagine to fill the gap. Those dreams and desires, however fantastical, speak to and keep in circulation the possibility of other, better ways of being. We do not need to speculate about a hard-wired utopian impulse in order to recognize that cultures throughout history and across the globe are suffused with utopian hopes and dreams. Christian narratives imagine a return to the innocence of Eden or the journey to a paradise after death. Folksongs, poems and paintings depict worlds of sensual satisfaction, lands of Cokaygne in which bodily desires are immediately fulfilled (Sargent 1994). Novels detail the structures of an ideal commonwealth or a perfect technocracy; fantasy films draw us into images of vivid unspoilt natural landscapes that speak of a simpler and more fulfilling existence. Adverts suggest that happiness is a new kitchen; political parties promise a brighter future. Utopianism is at work across politics and popular culture and linked with experiential and affective aspects of ordinary experience (Anderson 2006a, 2006b).

The argument that utopian hope and anticipation is part of the fabric of everyday life was powerfully and persuasively developed by the German philosopher Ernst Bloch. In *The Principle of Hope* (1986), Bloch identified utopian impulses at work in literature, religion and high art, but also in people's idle daydreams, in advertising, in the desires inculcated and organized by commodity capitalism. Utopian images of the good life are part of the hope mobilized by communist, fascist and nationalist movements. For Bloch, both human experience and social reality are always unfinished. Anticipatory consciousness and an orientation towards the future are part of the human psyche; likewise, the material reality that shapes us is incomplete, always unfolding. Bloch insists that utopia is not something transcendent, outside ordinary experience. It does not require a special epistemology to access the possibility of things being otherwise. The desire for a different and better way of being does not require the full-blown projection of an alternative (Gardiner 2001; Cooper 2014). Utopias are not (only) esoteric visions or projections confined between the covers of a book; they are part of our social, cultural and imaginative equipment.

For Bloch, utopias mattered most insofar as they kept alive the possibility of an unalienated existence. As a Marxist philosopher and critical theorist, for Bloch this entailed the restoration of human subjects to freedom from material conditions of alienated labour and the ideological prison of the commodity fetish. He sought to identify and add to the currents in history that would lead from the oppression and exploitation under capitalism to the universal freedom of socialism. While Bloch's unwavering commitment to the concrete utopia of communism is now difficult to embrace, his insistence that both history and human beings are unfinished and unfulfilled, existing in a state of becoming and therefore open to an unfolding not-yet, remains invaluable for thinking about and thinking with utopias, and for understanding what utopianism might do to and for us. Bloch suggests that in periods of acute transformation, societies generate a profusion of images and narratives of freedom and alternative social arrangements that continue to suffuse cultures and keep alive the possibility of radical change even in less tumultuous times.

Bloch's work, along with that of Bauman (2000, 2003, 2009 [1976]) and Levitas (2010 [1990], 2013), also highlights the irreducibly social nature of utopias and utopianism. Utopias are doubly social. They are a product of, expressive of, particular social conditions, and they are about the possibility of a transformed society. The content of any utopian expression is irreducibly shaped by its social context. Utopias appear to be about an elsewhere or an alternative future – but the very act of imagining otherwise points to problems, lacks and issues in the present. Utopias reveal what is wrong with the societies we have. Jameson goes so far as to argue that utopias are only and entirely about the present and its limits. Rooted in a Marxist reading of culture as ultimately constrained by capitalist ideology, he argues that 'even our wildest imaginings are hostage...to our mode of production' (2005: xiii). Utopia, then, cannot create genuinely new or other ideas; 'at best' it serves 'the negative purpose of making us more aware of our mental and ideological imprisonment' in a complex socio-economic totality (2005: xii).

But even if the utopian imagination is limited by what is thinkable within current social and cultural horizons, it nonetheless has the capacity to work critically and creatively with that material. As a minimum, the articulation of utopian alternatives opposes and resists the widespread idea that major social transformation is not possible. It therefore functions to unsettle the status quo. Indeed, for many utopian theorists it is precisely this function that defines utopia (Suvin 1979; Moylan 1986; Levitas 2010 [1990]). On these readings, utopias temporarily unmoor reality from its overwhelming sense of taken-for-grantedness. They gesture towards the possibility of another way of being. As Levitas has argued (2010 [1990]), this can be a conservative or escapist moment: utopian dreaming can console or compensate us for a difficult reality. But utopias always have the capacity to estrange us from the social arrangements we inhabit, to contest the idea that they are necessary and even normal. Utopias imply that any given set of social, cultural and political structures are contingent and therefore changeable. Their function is critical: they offer a negative reflection on what is.[1]

Utopia is a very particular – perhaps even peculiar – kind of critique, however. Utopias do not merely say 'that's wrong', or 'that's unfair', or 'that makes people unhappy'. They express critique through the detailed imagination of or momentary desire for an alternative. Utopias say '*this* would be right' and 'men and women would be more equal if work were rearranged *thus*' and 'happiness feels like *that*'. Utopias describe or indicate 'the look and feel and shape and experiences of what an alternative might and could actually be' (Fitting 1998: 14). In gesturing at alternatives, utopias are creative, expressive and affirmative (Sargisson 2012). As Moylan argues, citing Badiou, utopian figurations offer a 'supplement or "going beyond" the current situation, the "what there is" '. They therefore invite us to seriously contemplate another way of being (Moylan 2011: 29).

In some social and historical contexts, the expression of desire for a better world is highly valued and the production of detailed plans for alternative societies flourishes. In early modernity the emergence of the natural sciences generated a spate of formal utopias; More's *Utopia* (1965 [1516]) gave a name to the literary genre and began a tradition of thinking about this paradoxical thing, the 'good place' that is nowhere. Enlightenment thinking and later progressive currents in Western democracies were also extremely hospitable to the utopian imagination. The eighteenth and nineteenth centuries saw a proliferation of utopian political programmes, movements and novels. Important voices in the emerging social and political sciences were proudly forward-looking, with a faith in the power of positive knowledge to uncover laws of social development that would enable rational minds to build a more fair and more just future (Kumar 1987; Levitas 2013). By the mid-twentieth century, however, utopia had become a much less comfortable idea, associated with totalitarian programmes from fascism to communism. There was a sense that modernity had brought violence and inhumanity as much as prosperity and progress.

Against this apparent retreat from utopia, the 1960s and 1970s saw a revival of utopian thought in politics and culture (Kumar 1987; Levitas 2008). It was strongly associated with new social movements – the countercultural left, second-wave feminism and nascent environmentalism. It was also marked by discomfort with the confident progressive ideologies of modernity, especially insofar as they were tied to capitalist projects of economic expansion and narrow models of liberal individual freedom. Rejecting rigid blueprints for social improvement, the new utopianism was reflexive and critical (Moylan 1986; Bammer 1991). My analysis of the history of environmental utopianism begins with ideas rooted in this period. It ends in our current time of what Bauman has called 'liquid' modernity (2000), an era committed to change but only for the sake of change – open-ended, never settling, driven by restless currents of globalization, projects for personal improvement, and the aggressive expansion of capitalism. In such contexts, many argue, collective utopian visions and goals disappear, or play only a muted counterpoint to wider discourses of cynicism, despair and indifference. Utopianism is colonized by capitalist logics; desire is attached to commodities; future dreams become individualized lifestyle aspirations (Levitas 2000; Bauman 2003; Jameson 2005; Thompson 2013). Utopias must reinvent themselves in a 'post-political' era wherein technocracy and management squeeze out the spaces of contestation and demands for fundamental change (Wilson and Swyngedouw 2015). In such contexts, dreams of a better life might become only the 'cruel optimism' that Berlant discusses (2011). Attachment to utopian desires, written in the language of post-war liberal visions of the good life but cut off from material and social opportunities to achieve them, might now be the cause of pain and a block to real fulfilment and freedom.

All the features of utopianism that I have discussed above help us to understand environmental utopias. We can see that utopias persist but change what Levitas (2010 [1990]) calls their form and function. In some periods there is explicit hope for a sustainable future; at other times fear, doubt and indifference seem more dominant. Seeing utopias as ubiquitous directs our attention beyond formal blueprints to identify multiple expressions of green hope. Understanding utopianism as a process of estrangement from taken-for-granted social arrangements makes clear that there cannot be a single utopia of sustainability but rather a range of ideas, expressed in diverse forms, about how we can live better with the natures we have and have made. The idea that utopias respond to and articulate lack is particularly important (Levitas 2010 [1990]). As Soper explains (2000), consumer capitalism appears to offer choices that can fulfil all desires. But it cannot offer a world in which objects are not reduced to their economic and instrumental values, and in which human well-being is not tied to consumption. Similarly, imaginations and epistemologies in modern and postmodern contexts have refused or struggled to articulate a world that is not relentlessly separated into nature and culture, humans and environment. Acknowledging that utopianism responds to specific social and historical contexts helps us to think carefully about the changing content, form and significance of green utopias during a period when environmental issues have shifted from the radical margins of public debate to the political and popular mainstream.

Ideal natures: entanglements of environment and utopia

The distinctiveness of utopia as a mode of thought depends both on the impulse to imagine a better way of living and the capacity to add some kind of substance to the notion of 'better'. Utopias communicate a sense of *how* life might be improved, how societies might be more usefully, ethically or beautifully arranged. When we articulate (implicitly or explicitly) what a good or better world might consist of, nature often comes into the picture. The ideal of a better life in harmony with the natural environment is common in Western cultural history (Pepper 1984; Soper 1995). In Judeo-Christian traditions, the very idea of a good or moral life emerges from Edenic visions of innocent humans at one with the giving, abundant, unspoilt Earth of God's creation. For Merchant (2003), Eden myths have been among the most powerful narrative lenses through which Western and particularly American societies have understood their relationship to their environments. Such narratives are powerfully nostalgic. In their most recognizable form they tell a backward-looking story of innocence lost, of unalienated and liberated existence before a fall, of better times in the past when humans were part of nature. Even when they look forward with hope to a better world to come, the goal of Eden narratives is restoration and return rather than the desire for something genuinely radical or new.

Christian narratives, along with classical myths and literatures, suffuse pre-modern cultures with pastoral utopian tropes wherein the good life is innocent and lived in harmony with a pure and enriching nature. In modernity the relationship between nature, human well-being and the good life is fundamentally rewritten. Modernity can be characterized as a decisive shift away from the state of nature in both material and epistemological terms. It promised a new understanding and control of nature through scientific knowledge.

The Enlightenment ushered in social and political systems devised by science and rational thought and responsive to democratic ideals of individual human rights and representation, no longer in thrall to tradition and faith in a divine or natural order. Industrial capitalism relied on a newly expansive capacity to exploit natural resources to generate material abundance and profit. Many environmentalist thinkers characterize modernity precisely in terms of the increasingly distant relationship of humans from the natural world – and argue that these are the ultimate roots of the environmental crisis that became visible in the twentieth century. But they also note a counter-tradition to powerful discourses and ideologies of technocentric instrumentalism and control. In transcendentalist philosophy and religion, in Romantic aesthetics, in nature writing and pastoral socialism, oppositional voices in culture and politics have called from the early days of modernity for the value of nonhuman nature and for the idea that human experience and subjectivity are enhanced by the capacity to experience and make connections with wild nature.

De Geus works through these complicated currents to identify two opposing utopian traditions in modernity with contrasting ideas about the relationship between nature and human societies. He argues that 'utopias of abundance' have dominated in Western culture, counterposed by a minor tradition of 'utopias of sufficiency' (De Geus 1999: 21–2). Progressive anthropocentric dreams of expansion and growth have been central to the forward-looking currents of modernity. In these utopias, the good life for humans is envisaged in terms of the instrumental and industrial exploitation of natural resources to generate surplus. Environmentalist thinkers argue that these attitudes cause environmental chaos and damage human well-being. They create narrow, consumerist ways of life that lack connections with others and with nature. Utopias of sufficiency envisage instead modest, careful ways of life that value proximity to nature and conserving resources. De Geus discusses variants of this tradition going back to More's *Utopia* with its vision of enough for all but excess for no-one. He examines Thoreau's idealization of solitary simplicity, Kropotkin's proposals for an anarchist-ecological state, Morris's pastoral vision of socialism in *News from Nowhere*, 1905, Howard's plans for garden cities, and twentieth-century green utopian fictions including Huxley's *Island*, 1962, and Callenbach's *Ecotopia*, 1975. De Geus traces an unbroken thread of desire for a modest way of life in communion with the natural environment that contests modernity's expansionist ambitions and offers an alternative vision for a sustainable future.

De Geus's work has been valuable in identifying key features of ecological utopianism in modernity. But I don't think it is helpful to think of green utopias as an unbroken countermelody to modernity's utopias of technocentrism and expansion. They are constantly reinvented in response to changing historical contexts. Although some elements of the values on which ecotopian visions are based endure, the structures and lifestyles of their imagined societies change over time, as do the forms in which they are expressed. I think it is also a mistake to assume that ecocentric visions are necessarily critical and progressive. Nature often acts as an object of concern and a source of value and human transformation in explicitly utopian green visions. But nature is a complex, slippery and problematic concept in Western cultures. Images and ideas about the intrinsic value of the environment can be used to naturalize human relationships, presenting contingent and unequal socio-economic arrangements as eternal and somehow necessary. Looking 'back' to nature for models of human well-being can be socially regressive and politically conservative. European traditions of representing natural landscapes, both textually and in the visual arts, have been accused of presenting a mythical vision of an unspoilt countryside that distorts classed experiences and glosses difficult questions of property ownership (Cosgrove 1988; McNaghten and Urry 1998). Nature all too often serves ideological purposes, and nature utopias can circulate in support of reactionary and compensatory visions as well as progressive and critical ones.

The emergence of the figure of environmental crisis in the 1970s marked a new phase in Western ideas about the relationship between social practices, the natural world, and human well-being. The environmentalist movements that emerged in this period shared many ideas about the need to protect and value nature with older narratives and ideals. These include notions of human stewardship drawn from

Christian traditions; Romantic ideas of the value of wilderness and the capacity of individual subjects to be transformed by their connection with wild nature; and pastoral ideals of a balanced, harmonious existence deeply rooted in a particular place. But post-war environmentalism also reshaped those ideas in response to new challenges. It developed its own concepts and approaches. Contemporary environmentalism owes as much to ecosystems science as to the Romantics. It introduced a novel sense of the planetary scale of environmentalism problems and their consequences. It developed distinctive understandings of the systematic ways in which global socio-economic systems impact on the environment. The environmentalist movements of the 1970s responded to a particular set of socio-economic conditions in Europe and the US: increasingly mobile and volatile capitalist accumulation; pollution and resource depletion on a new scale; relative affluence and the consumer society; perceived social problems of alienation and atomization. The extensive and intensive debates about the future of human/natural relationships that emerged in contemporary environmentalism were new in scope, content and epistemology (Eyerman and Jamison 1991; Dobson 1995; Jamison 2001).

In this book I treat the relationship between contemporary environmentalism and utopianism as a particularly intense and interesting one. Firstly, the preoccupation of post-war environmentalism with systemic environmental problems meant that it often imagined wholesale alternatives to the status quo. Formal, prescriptive visions – tellingly, often called blueprints – proliferated in environmentalist discourse from the 1970s, detailing the structures and arrangements of a more sustainable society. Secondly, environmentalist discourses are strongly extrapolative, looking ahead to different nature-futures in order to evaluate existing structures and practices. Dominant environmentalist narratives projected looming catastrophe and collapse. But that 'apocalyptic horizon' (Dryzek 1997: 37) also opened up possibilities for imagining alternatives. Rejecting the business as usual that would lead us into ecological disaster, environmentalism created new cultural spaces for exploring better futures with nature. Finally, in the more visionary and philosophical strands of post-war environmentalism, there is a strong metaphysical dimension (Eckersley 1992) which resonates with utopian desire and radicalism. Ecological philosophy and critique undertook a thorough re-evaluation of the meaning and significance of nature, generating new utopian ethics for protecting and valuing it, and utopian proposals for enhancing human well-being by returning to it. In all these ways, the emergence of new environmentalist ideas in the 1960s and 1970s was infused with powerfully utopian elements.

This environmental utopianism depended on ecocentric values and ideals that grounded hope for a better future in the need to protect and return to a separate nature. More recently, however, ideas that question the very existence and value of nature have begun to circulate, intensified by contemporary understandings of anthropogenic climate change and predictions of its effects. Some thinkers, including prominent environmentalists, argue that the natural world is now so threatened and contaminated by human activities that it cannot act as a source of value and hope for the future. Others suggest that the category of nature stands in the way of a more thorough and radical rethinking of human/ environmental relationships. These arguments about the end of nature are, I think, a new and important part of the constantly changing relationship between utopia and contemporary environmentalism. They are accompanied by a pervasive sense, also intimately related to the dynamics and cultural representation of climate change, that it is no longer possible to imagine better futures. The end of nature and the end of the future do not spell the end of green utopias. But they do suggest a new phase of changes in their content, form and function.

Before and after the end of nature

In this book I look at different strands of green utopianism in Western and particularly Anglophone environmentalism, ecological philosophy and speculative fiction since the 1960s. I examine distinct clusters of green utopian ideas and situate them in their socio-historical contexts. The discussion is framed by the changing trajectory of environmental politics over the last forty years (Jamison 2001; Dobson 2009; Wapner 2010), showing how its developing entanglement with popular culture and mainstream politics has shaped successive green future visions. I separate contemporary Western green hope analytically into two phases. The first part of the book (chapters 2–4) explores the first, focusing on the alternative values and utopian hopes that responded in the 1970s to fears of environmental catastrophe and to the threat of ecological limits to socio-economic growth. From the 1980s to the mid-1990s, environmentalism became more mainstream, and sustainable development became the dominant policy framework for thinking about environmental futures. At the same time, philosophers argued for radically ecocentric values and produced visions of societies re-embedded in their natural ecosystems. These ideas were elaborated and developed into vivid and affective critical (Moylan 1986) green utopian fiction from the mid-1970s to the mid-1990s.

This period saw the emergence of an urgent and revelatory environmentalism which sought to put the future of nature on the public agenda. Environmental concern was driven by a need to critically re-appraise dominant capitalist models of social and economic development, demonstrate their impact on the natural environment and human well-being, and show that alternatives were possible. Environmental campaigners argued that although nature was threatened, it could be saved. Green utopias flourished, and radically new visions of human well-being and the good society emerged. Since the 1990s, however, the political and social contexts of environmentalist ideas have shifted. Environmental concerns have been normalized in Western societies, internalized into mainstream politics and capitalist enterprise (Jamison 2001; Buell 2003). Some argue that this has been a positive process of ecological modernization, whereby institutions and ideologies adapt in order to address the environmental risks and problems that they have generated. Others argue instead that we have entered an era of post-environmental politics – or even a post-political era – in which public discourse and popular spectacle intensify around environmental problems, but little action is taken to address them. At the same time, the environmental concerns we face have grown in number and severity.

In chapters 5 and 6 I explore the second phase, asking what has happened to green utopianism as environmental politics has entered the mainstream and as climate change has become an increasingly visible threat to a sustainable future. Global warming is now widely accepted as the outcome of human-social processes already set in train over past decades and centuries. Scientific consensus on the anthropogenic origins of climate change has, for many, fundamentally changed our environmental predicament, and even the world we live in. It has become more difficult to believe that the future will be fundamentally different from the present – and for the future to function as a space for imagining alternatives. It becomes easier to believe that environmental apocalypse is inevitable or already unfolding. A second phase of green utopianism then comes in some sense (materially or conceptually) after nature. Some argue that we are facing the loss of physical nature as something separate from humanity (Buell 2003; McKibben 2003 [1989]). Others argue that this nature never existed, and we should speed up the loss of a category of human thought which only ever reflected the binary habits of modernity and left us incapable of recognizing the hybrid world we really inhabit (Latour 2004; Bennett 2010; Morton 2010). In these contexts, appeals to saving or getting back to nature become problematic as the basis for green hopes and desires. Formal environmentalist utopias are thin on the ground. In the literary sphere, post-apocalyptic and dystopian fictions proliferate.

Each chapter explores a set of interlinked developments in the green utopian imagination in loosely chronological order. The first three chapters explore three different aspects of the green hope of the first phase of Western environmentalism in terms of the distinctive utopian values they expressed and the forms and functions that utopianism took. Chapter 2 looks at popular environmentalism in the 1970s. Its future visions extrapolated expansionist and technocratic trends in socio-economic life to show their potential to produce catastrophic ecological and social consequences. At the same time, it sketched novel no-growth alternatives. The chapter also explores how, as global environmental policy visions developed into the 1980s, the model of sustainable development came to envisage a future in which economic growth could be reconciled with environmental security. Chapter 3 examines deep ecological philosophy to show how it treated environmental crisis as an opportunity for social renewal and the exploration of new models of human well-being. Chapter 4 looks at how science fiction responded to and thoroughly reworked radical ecological ideas in the mid-1970s to the mid-1990s to offer vivid explorations of life in a sustainable society. I look at fictional works by Marge Piercy, Ursula K. Le Guin and Kim Stanley Robinson.

The last two substantive chapters look at a later phase of green hope. Chapter 5 considers mainstream responses to global warming in the early twenty-first century. It attempts to trace utopian moments among and in contrast to both the apocalyptic rhetorics and narratives of no future that have shaped climate projections, and the mainstream environmental policy responses that privilege small behavioural changes, technological modifications and manageable targets. Chapter 6 traces a related set of concerns emerging through the same period. Some philosophical responses to current environmental dilemmas suggest that we face the end of nature. For some we are living through a physical loss of nature, demanding a response marked by grief and the humble constraint of human desires. Others celebrate the end of nature, arguing that it opens up the utopian prospect of a new and better understanding of our hybrid world. In each chapter I look at how speculative fiction has continued to explore and express the possibility of green hope even as carbon futures shrink into the present and the idea of a return to a more natural way of living and being becomes either untenable or undesirable. In chapter 5 I focus on how science fiction has re-imagined utopia in terms of process and adaptation, and how apocalyptic figures open up radical spaces of green desire against the normalization of environmental crisis. In chapter 6 I look at changing depictions of landscapes and spaces in green speculative fictions which shift from images of natural to postnatural. I explore how, increasingly framed by narratives of loss, utopian hope shifts into modes of mourning and the uncanny.

Each chapter looks closely at a particular set of green ideas and how they shape proposals for a better social relationship with the natural world. I look at the content of those visions, but also at the contexts and debates that generate them and at how they are expressed. As the meanings of environment and environmentalism change, we need to look for expressions of green hope and desire in different places. I use a broad definition of utopias and utopianism that extends green desires for a better way of living and being beyond literary eco-utopias, green communes and environmentalist political tracts. I look at how green utopianism circulates through Western cultures in a variety of forms. In the early days of environmental movements, utopianism was often explicit, direct and highly visible in the public imagination. In the 1970s popular scientific publications rehearsed ideas about the alternatives to growth and books about the limits of Western industrial social systems sold in millions. Blueprints for green alternatives proliferated, detailing new social structures for sustainability. These ideas both inspired and were transformed by green utopian fictions that were widely read.

Detailed images of sustainable societies are not currently conspicuous in mainstream environmentalism. Environmental messages continue to circulate, but the space for overtly utopian imaginaries seems to have shrunk. Projections of green futures are more likely to take the form of apocalyptic climate predictions, dystopian explorations of human survival through slow environmental disintegration. There is a widespread sense of the impossibility of mitigating systemic environmental problems. But expressions of desire for a greener world and a more sustainable way of living remain a feature of contemporary culture and politics. They do not take the form of traditional utopian blueprints – optimistic, forward-looking plans for new societies. Contemporary environmental utopianism operates in amongst pessimistic, apocalyptic or pragmatic tropes. It often emerges against the grain, as an echo or desiring trace, framed by fears for the loss of nature and half-hidden in nostalgia and mourning. Contemporary green utopianism is often expressed in images rather than words, often entangled in commodified desires rather than clearly in opposition to them. But it continues to function as a vital space for the cultivation of new ecological values and desires, for the imagination of alternative social forms, and for the emergence of new models of human well-being.

The environmental humanities, literary ecocriticism and green cultural studies are now generating plentiful resources for analysing how ideas about nature circulate via narrative (Coupe 2000; Buell 2003; Garrard 2011; Otto 2012; Canavan and Robinson 2014), film (Ivakhiv 2013; Brereton 2015; Rust et al. 2015) and indeed across media, arts and cultural practice (*inter alia* Hochman 1988; Szerszynski et al. 2004; Skrimshire 2010b; Doyle 2011; Gabrys and Yusoff 2011; Heffernan and Wragg 2011; Morton 2013). More recently, literary and cultural critics have been using the contested idea of the Anthropocene to explore how culture is representing an apparent shift into a new era with monumental consequences for our ideas about the world we live in and our own agency (Clark 2015; Purdy 2015; Trexler 2015; Wark 2015). This may seem fanciful or pointless in the face of pressing warnings about dramatic climate change and the imminent loss of species and biodiversity. But neither mainstream environmental policy-making nor radical activism have thus far succeeded in turning around the systematic and increasing unsustainability of global economic systems. Few of us in the global North are making significant changes in our daily lives. In this context of disempowerment, indifference and painfully slow change, we need to look hard at our culture to see how it is shaping our sense of the future. There is room for consideration of how we can cultivate and educate desires for a better, greener future. We need to think about what kind of future we want, not just what kind of future we expect to happen.

This book suggests that taking utopia seriously is one way that we can learn how to look anew at our future with nature and to imagine it differently. It also suggests that the ideas and narratives that can help us to do that are already circulating in contemporary politics and culture. Eminent sociologists and social geographers have begun to invite their disciplines to become more explicitly speculative (Harvey 2000; Giddens 2011; Urry 2011), constructing scenarios of sustainable and post-carbon future societies and examining and popularizing them as part of a wider public debate about environmental and climate crisis – and what comes after. But social scientists sometimes overlook the extent to which that work is already being done by polemicists, film-makers, newspaper headline writers – and especially science fiction authors. Green futures and green utopias are always already at work. Although often limited, they can be a creative and vital form of cultural speculation and critique. They indicate the discursive limits of the present and help to educate desires for a greener society. Thus they ought to be an important object of sociological interest. But utopias can also be a vital form of lay sociology, offering critical analyses of existing social structures and speculative visions of alternatives. Sociology can learn from utopianism (Levitas 2013), as well as by studying utopias.

In order to develop greener worlds, we will need to unsettle capitalist models of value and create alternative ways of understanding how we produce and consume nature. We will have to challenge binary epistemologies and come up with new ways of grasping the hybridity of life, human and nonhuman. If we are to live more generously, more richly, more ethically with multiple ecologies and nonhuman others, we will need to re-imagine metaphysics in terms of connections, hybrids and networks (Latour 2004). The critical, unsettling and creative powers of utopianism add to our capacity to change the way we see and interact with the wider cosmos. Recently, scholars in utopian studies have begun to think of utopia less as an object or a thing, and more as a method (Moylan and Baccolini 2007; Levitas 2013). Utopia is seen as a heuristic, an interpretative tool or an epistemological mode which insists that what is is always already shot through with ideas about what could and should be. The utopian method can, as Levitas (2013) puts it, help to dig up and criticize implicit ideas about the good life and human nature in apparently objective, neutral and practical ideas (what Levitas calls the archaeological and ontological modes of the utopian method). It can also help us develop a more explicit commitment to speculation about probable, possible and desirable futures in the human and social sciences (Levitas's architectural mode). This book traces some of the work that green utopias have already done. In the face of apocalyptic, despairing or indifferent responses to contemporary ecological dilemmas, utopias and the utopian method seem more necessary than ever.

2

Environmentalism: From Crisis to Hope

If the present growth trends in world population, indus-trialization, pollution, food production and resource depletion continue unchanged, the limits to growth on this planet will be reached sometime within the next one hundred years. The probable result will be a rather sudden and uncontrollable decline in population and industrial capacity. (Meadows et al. 1972: 23)

Our report...is not a prediction of ever increasing envi-ronmental decay, poverty and hardship in an ever more polluted world among ever decreasing resources. We see instead the possibility for a new era of economic growth, one based on policies that sustain and expand the environmental resource base. (WCED 1987: 1)

Whole earth, new futures

In the early 1970s a number of texts and ideas emerged that would prove critically important in the development of new frameworks for thinking about green futures. In 1970, *Time* magazine announced the arrival of an environmental crisis.

That year also saw the first Earth Day, and the foundation of the US Environmental Protection Agency. In 1972, the first United Nations Conference on the Human Environment was held, followed by the founding of the United Nations Environment Programme. The Club of Rome's *Limits to Growth* report, cited above, made a powerful intervention into global economic policy discourse. James Lovelock and Lynn Margulis first stated the Gaia hypothesis. In 1973, against the backdrop of the oil crisis and growing fears about the availability of natural resources, E.F. Schumacher set out a new model for economics 'as if people mattered' (Schumacher 1993 [1973]), and Herman Daly edited a collection of essays about the possibility of a steady-state economy (1973). Concerns about the long-term prospects for humanity and increasing damage to and depletion of the natural environment, growing in visibility throughout the 1960s, were reaching a new intensity.[1] There was a sense that the world was facing systemic ecological problems whose root cause was the industrial capitalist way of life.

These ideas about nature were framed by the scientific study of ecology, which emphasized the interrelatedness of elements in an ecosystem. Systems thinking more broadly was related to new forms of large-scale data analyses enabled by computers, leading to new ways of looking at the relationship between human populations and the natural resources they depend on. Drawing on both of these developments, mainstream environmentalism from the 1970s onwards was marked by two distinct elements. The first was a sense of planetary scale. Since the late 1960s, the US moon landings had been generating images of earth seen from space. As these novel images circulated through popular culture, the icon of the blue planet became a powerful signifier for environmental awareness (Sachs 1994). It suggested a planet that was beautiful, rich and fertile, yet singular and fragile. Ecological concerns were being rewritten at a global scale, and the fate of all humankind seemed to lie in the balance. The second element was a logic of extrapolation which sought to imagine future outcomes of continuing socio-economic patterns, and use them to change things in the present. The epistemological and moral fibre of early environmentalism was intimately tied up with its 'clear set of theses about the future' (Ross 1991: 184).

The early 1970s saw many attempts to construct future scenarios by projecting current trends in resource use, pollution and population growth. Environmentalism was full of 'futurologists, planners, forecasters and model-builders' (Schumacher 1993 [1973]: 186). Analysts tried to understand the way the whole global system was heading, one eye on the health of environmental systems and the other on the increasing demands placed on those systems by an expanding human population and unprecedented levels of consumption in Western economies. The extrapolative hypothetical futures that emerged in this period were on the whole dire. If things went on unchanged, we faced the collapse of global ecosystems with economic and social chaos to follow. Business as usual was no longer an option. The emergence of modern environmentalism in Western societies came wrapped up in the language of imminent crisis. Books talked about a 'population bomb' and the 'predicament of mankind' [sic]. Dryzek has called this 'apocalyptic horizon' the key feature of environmentalist discourse in the period (1997: 37). Progress along the lines of industrial expansion, consumerism and population growth could only lead to catastrophe.

But if modern environmentalism was founded on looking ahead to the prospect of a disastrous future, it also made room for the imagination of better alternatives. Extrapolations of the catastrophic consequences of current practices showed what would happen if things went on. The 'if' in that formulation also launched visions of very different socioeconomic alternatives. In this chapter I examine some of the main ideas from this phase of environmentalist concern. I focus on well-known texts that were widely read at the time and are seen retrospectively as having made a significant conceptual contribution to constructing what came to be known as the environmental crisis. They are the Club of Rome's *The Limits to Growth* (Meadows et al. 1972), whose key ideas are set out in the quote at the beginning of this chapter, Schumacher's (1993 [1973]) *Small is Beautiful*, and *The Ecologist*'s *A Blueprint for Survival* (1973). Taken together, these texts constructed a radical and popular environmental discourse. It combined the newly insistent metaphysics of a single finite planet with epistemologies that emphasized the need to understand the world in terms of complex interlocking systems and the argument that there are biophysical limits to economic growth. A rhetorical focus on apocalypse also mobilized the possibility of alternatives. It made a new space for exploring green utopian desires and launched detailed visions for a more sustainable economy and society. Mainstream environmentalism and environmental policy no longer talks about limits to growth. The environmental problematic that emerged in the 1970s has undergone numerous changes, reflecting new scientific ideas, changing political and policy settlements, shifting institutional concerns, and new epistemologies of the natural and the social. One pivotal change was the shift from a dominant environmental storyline of limits to one of sustainable development that took place in the 1980s. Environmentalist discourse in the early 1970s was about the dramatic announcement of an environmental crisis. The very idea of limits to growth and the relentless reiteration of the prospects of catastrophe authorized the imagination of social renewal. Multiple visions of alternative futures were articulated by activists, maverick scientists and impromptu think tanks. By the mid-1980s, however, environmental concerns were becoming more mainstream and a new message was emerging. The public voices of environmentalism were becoming those of institutional actors affiliated to international governmental and non-governmental organizations (NGOs). Many were arguing that a greener future could be created by modifying and refining global economic growth, not by ending it. In 1987 *Our Common Future*, the report of the United Nations Environment Programme's World Commission on Environment and Development (WCED 1987) laid down the key terms of what would become the dominant global discourse of sustainable development throughout the 1980s and 1990s, seen in the second quote at the beginning of this chapter.

In the second section of this chapter, I focus on the formulation of sustainable development as a global policy goal. I trace the emergence of the discourse of sustainability and examine how it came to displace limits to growth as the key storyline of the environmental problematic. I look at the new logics of futurity laid out in *Our Common Future* (hereafter 'the Brundtland Report' after its lead author; WCED 1987). It replaced a rhetoric of environmental crisis and limits with one of development paths that would lead from present economic structures and practices towards a more environmentally secure future. The lens of utopian studies allows me to look closely and critically at how the discourse of sustainable development generated visions of a more careful, responsible and reflexive version of the industrial capitalist present. These visions were more optimistic than the limits discourse, but at the same time significantly less radical and visionary. Brundtland offered cautious hope for a sustainable future, but it also paved the way for environmentalism to invest in the continuation of economic growth. As well as the Brundtland Report, I look briefly at Agenda 21, the action plan for sustainable development that came out of the UN Conference on Environment and Development (UNCED) in Rio de Janeiro 1992 and framed national and international environment policies; one of its chapters outlined a Local Agenda 21 which launched thousands of local-level sustainable development initiatives through the 1990s.

This chapter works on and with what we might call different discourses of the environment (Hajer 1995; Dryzek 1997; Alexander 2010) or social constructions of environmental problems (Hannigan 2014). Discursive approaches insist that our understanding of environmental issues is shaped by the ways we represent them to ourselves. They focus on the organizing narratives and images that make environmental crisis real in the public imagination and frame organized responses to it. Here I explore the dominant environmental storylines in circulation from the early 1970s to roughly the mid-1990s. These discourses have been widely discussed in the decades since. What I add to this debate is a focus on the different kinds of future scenarios and utopian hopes generated within different articulations of the environmental problematic. I draw on Torgerson's detailed exploration of the construction of different kinds of futures for nature and society within the limits and sustainable development paradigms respectively, and I reiterate his argument that the shift from one to the other was the most significant development in environmentalist discourse in the second half of the twentieth century (Torgerson 1995, 1999; see also McManus 1996; Irwin 2001; Blewitt 2014). I focus on how this reshapes the possibilities for green utopianism. In the next chapter

I consider the more radical discourses and philosophies of ecological thinkers. Here I am interested in the mainstream: the shaping of the centre ground, the ideas that dominated media and policy discussions.

The limits to growth and the apocalyptic horizon[2]

> We do not need to destroy utterly the ecosphere to bring catastrophe upon ourselves; all we have to do is to carry on as we are, clearing forests, 'reclaiming' wetlands, and imposing sufficient quantities of pesticides, radioactive materials, plastic, sewage and industrial wastes upon our air, water and land systems to make them inhospitable to the species on which their continued integrity and stability depend.
> (*The Ecologist* 1973: 22)

In 1972 *The Limits to Growth: A Report for the Club of Rome on the Predicament of Mankind* announced that a looming crisis threatened both global ecosystems and socio-economic security. The report was commissioned by the Club of Rome, a kind of international think tank founded by European scientists and economists. It was written and researched by academics in systems management, business schools and environmental science at MIT. It carried the authority and cachet of mainstream science and reached millions of readers. *The Limits to Growth* articulated a new 'world problematique' (Meadows et al. 1972: 10), stimulated popular debate about environmental conditions, and helped to put questions of environment and development on the international political and policy agenda. It was part of the articulation of a novel environmental storyline that re-ordered understandings of social relationships with nature and thereby opened up new conditions for the exercise of the green utopian imagination.

The report's message, as can be seen from the quote above, was that unlimited economic growth would inevitably hit up against the earth's finite ecological carrying capacity. Expanding production and global population growth were putting unprecedented pressures on natural ecosystems. Economic progress was beginning to cause systematic environmental breakdown. The report drew its dramatic conclusions from the results of computer modelling of a 'world system' (Meadows et al. 1972: 5). Data on five key variables – population, food supply, industrialization, pollution and depletion of non-renewable resources – was modelled to generate 100-year future scenarios (Meadows et al. 1972: 21). A standard run assumed the continuation of current rates of economic development, resource use, population growth and food production. It predicted rapid depletion of non-renewable resources, followed by sharp price rises, the collapse of the industrial base and food production, then rapid population decline. In short, economic business as usual would lead to 'overshoot and collapse in both ecological and socio-economic systems' (Meadows et al. 1972: 126). In subsequent runs, variables were altered but produced equally dismal results. Factoring in the discovery of new stocks of non-renewable resources led to new rounds of economic growth, sharp increases in pollution, depletion of the agricultural base, and collapse of human populations. Factoring in new technologies that could absorb pollution only led to faster depletion of non-renewable resources and the same stark ending. The report was insistent that there could be no technological fix for overshoot and collapse.

Limits was subjected to criticism from the moment it appeared, especially by optimistic liberal economists who condemned the Club of Rome's Malthusian pessimism and insisted on the essential resourcefulness of both humans and planet (Simon and Kahn 1984). Many took issue with the data sets that fed the computer models. Others questioned the outcomes that they generated. Some focused on the epistemological assumptions of the whole project, suggesting that complex and diverse environmental, economic and social systems relationships could not be reduced to quantitative variables and then modelled to generate meaningful predictions. Others suggested that detailed hypothetical models were an unnecessarily 'elaborate' route to reach the rather straightforwardly self-evident insight that 'infinite growth of material consumption in a finite world is an impossibility' (Schumacher 1993 [1973]: 98). As Schumacher suggests, the significance of *The Limits to Growth* is its conceptual claim that ecosystems cannot indefinitely support unlimited economic growth and rapid population expansion. The idea that there are absolute limits to growth rewrote the environmental storyline in the early 1970s. The report suggested that there is a systematic link between the ideologies of progress at the heart of industrial capitalism and growing environmental pollution and depletion. It argued that the apparent success of progress, usually measured by economic growth (at the national level gross domestic product), in fact constitutes a deep failure in terms of environmental protection and conservation and a risk to future human security and well-being. If progress depends on the systematic exploitation of natural resources to provide material wealth, *Limits* argues, the current Western way of life cannot continue.

Two features of the world system model underpinning the Club of Rome's claims were particularly important. The first was that it looked at interrelationships and feedback loops between variables in a closed system. *Limits* offered a powerful instantiation of the ecological idea that social and natural processes at the global scale are locked together in a highly responsive, multi-faceted knot. All elements have consequences for the others and for the system as a whole. Thus the only rational way to think about the future is by looking at the whole system. The second feature was the assertion that world population and industrial systems were growing exponentially. Exponential growth is growth at a constant percentage rate of the whole over a given time period. Compared to linear growth (a constant amount over a given time period), exponential growth produces dramatic rather than incremental changes because of the doubling built in at the end. The most commonly given example of this effect is the pond in which a lily pad is increasing its size by 100% every day. One day the pond is only half full; the next it is completely covered (Meadows et al. 1972: 30; Dobson 1995: 76).

In systems characterized by multiple, complex feedback loops and subject to exponential growth, there is a 'false sense of security' that an existing state can continue indefinitely (*The Ecologist* 1973: 18). But change can be sudden and catastrophic; the future cannot be taken for granted. *The Limits to Growth* looked forward to a threshold, anticipated a radical break, and indicated the calamitous future that might follow. Sometime in the twenty-first century, human development would hit limits to growth and face ecological collapse and socio-economic crisis. The more prosperous Western societies became and the more widely industrial capitalist systems spread, the more likely the system would bring about its own end in resource exhaustion, rampant pollution and economic disaster. This is what Dryzek calls the 'apocalyptic horizon' (1997: 37) of limits discourse. Its understanding of the present and the need for action now is conditioned by a viewpoint fixed on a point of possible collapse just visible in the future. Dryzek also notes its metaphors of unfolding collapse, death and decay (Dryzek 1997: 36; see also Dobson 1995). Beyond the apocalyptic horizon lies a wasteland. These features all contributed to an understanding of the environmental problematic in the early 1970s as dramatic, urgent and global.

One response to the limits to growth thesis in the 1970s was a politically authoritarian discourse that Eckersley and others have called survivalism (Eckersley 1992; Dryzek 1997).[3] Survivalism argued that developed societies had become complacent in their expansionist ethos and argued for draconian authoritarian responses: for 'resource rationing, increasing government intervention, centralization, and population control' (Eckersley 1992: 13). Assuming rampant human self-interest and greed, survivalist politics argued that state and social control were needed to manage ecological limits. Solutions to the environmental problematic were framed in terms of control and coercion. The threat of catastrophic collapse was used rhetorically to restrict the space in which the future could be imagined to one of crisis aversion and conservation. In the context of the growth of authoritarian political rhetoric in the 1970s, it may seem strange to argue that the limits discourse was a rich seedbed for emancipatory and progressive green utopias. But it was. The Club of Rome's report not only predicted a desperate future; it also outlined desirable alternatives. Perhaps more importantly, the very logic of environmental crisis opened up new spaces in which the desires for new social, ethical and political possibilities could flourish. If the current system could not go on, the apocalyptic mode wonders what we might have coming to us. A closely associated utopian mode asks: what else might we choose?

The Limits to Growth used extrapolative models and rhetorics of discontinuity and crisis to create a space into which change and the possibility of different social-environmental alternatives could be projected. Crisis rhetoric presented a dramatic challenge to the assumption that the good life depended on ever-increasing economic growth. The possibility of overshoot and collapse contested the idea that the future must be like the present, only more so. The scenarios modelled in *The Limits to Growth* were not intended to foretell the future in any straightforward way. Rather they offered new ways of understanding business as usual and worked instead to problematize contemporary structures and dynamics. The idea of limits to growth makes the apparently 'unnatural and unimaginable' prospect of a stable and sustainable society conceivable (Meadows et al. 1972: 167). Within the limits discourse, the environmental crisis could be about thriving, not merely surviving.

The Club of Rome's report briefly sketched liberatory and emancipatory alternatives to bare survival and authoritarian controls. Its final chapter explored an 'equilibrium' economy[4] in which the drive for economic growth would be replaced by the maintenance of a dynamic balance of opposing forces (Meadows et al. 1972: 172). Overall population would be reduced by limiting births and economies would be slowed down by investing in production only at the rate of capital depreciation. For the Club of Rome, a no-growth economy did not mean the end of human and social development. Quite the opposite: the arts, sciences and interpersonal relationships could all be enhanced in societies in which material needs are met, where less time is dedicated to production and more to care and personal fulfilment (Meadows et al. 1972: 175). The report argued against the 'myth' that social justice depends on economic growth, and instead argued for income redistribution and greater economic equality (1972: 178). The report does not include a detailed utopian vision. But it does express utopian desires for an alternative world in which the basic needs of all would be met and everyone would have the opportunity for personal and social development. It tried to establish this goal as feasible, arguing that late twentieth-century societies possessed the technological, scientific, political and social resources needed to 'create a totally new form of human society' (p. 184).

Emancipatory alternatives to growth were also explored in Schumacher's *Small is Beautiful*, published the year after the Club of Rome's report and a highly influential text in environmental economics. Like *Limits*, it is mainly an extended diagnosis of the crises facing Western societies in the late twentieth century, and it blamed unchecked growth for chronic environmental problems. Less apocalyptic in tone than the Club of Rome's report, and less interested in the modelling of aggregate data sets, *Small is Beautiful* nonetheless extrapolated from current trends of growth a future riven by crises of pollution and resource depletion. Schumacher focused on the tendency of industrial systems to use up natural capital (non-renewable resources) as if it were income that could be replaced. Schumacher was also deeply concerned by what he saw as a spiritual crisis linked to economic materialism and the dehumanization of work in industrial societies, the 'hollowness and fundamental unsatisfactoriness of a life devoted to the pursuit of material ends' (1993 [1973]: 24). In the face of an industrial system that is failing humans as well as destroying nature, Schumacher insists that nothing short of a 'romantic, utopian vision' (1993 [1973]: 125) of happier, more fulfilling, more environmentally stable and less violent forms of social life is needed.

Schumacher's book differs from *Limits* in its exploration of concrete examples of the alternative social and technological systems that he endorses. Although inspired by Buddhist and Confucianist philosophy, and exploring prospects for 'metaphysical' change (1993 [1973]: 221), many of Schumacher's suggestions for alternatives are nonetheless reformist and practical. He suggests models for decentralized collective ownership of productive enterprises (1993 [1973]: 227), an alternative to both private share ownership and national and centralized public ownership, which according to Schumacher allowed producers to ignore local environmental and social consequences of industrial activity. He is critical of transnational corporations, and suggests that at a certain size all businesses should be 50% owned by the public, who would receive a dividend from profits in lieu of business taxes

(1993 [1973]: 242). Schumacher also urged the development of what he called intermediate technologies. Large-scale technologies of mass production undermine human skills and the pleasures of work at the same time as they risk causing enormous environmental problems. Alternative appropriate technologies enabling production by the masses would complement human skill and creativity, and remain accountable to local producers and communities.[5]

Limits to Growth and *Small is Beautiful*, then, were utopian in the expressive and desiring sense I outlined in chapter 1. The latter also offered examples of alternatives to growth economics and industrial capitalism and technology. But both Schumacher and the Club of Rome focused primarily on setting out a diagnosis of the environmental problematic. A formal and detailed utopian vision rooted in the limits discourse came with *The Ecologist* magazine's 'A Blueprint for Survival' in 1972 (*The Ecologist* 1973).[6] The Blueprint explicitly sought to provide 'proposals for creating a sustainable society' rather than offer 'yet another recitation of the reasons why this should be done' (1973: 14). It set out the main elements of an ecologically and economically stable society: minimal disruption of ecological processes; an 'economy of stock rather than flow'; and a population in which birth rates would be regulated at replacement level (*The Ecologist* 1973: 34). The Blueprint suggests a society dedicated to conservation of resources, a resurgence of craft skills and production for durability, even proposing taxes on raw materials and an amortization tax which would punish products with a short lifecycle and encourage production for longevity (*The Ecologist* 1973: 43–4). Stable societies would recycle, develop new forms of pollution control, establish organic agriculture and conserve wilderness. People would live in small, tightly integrated communities and learn to enjoy a lifestyle that was less mobile and more communal, less consumerist and more politically participatory. Across the world, population would be stabilized using humane methods including education, provision of contraception and cultural persuasion (1973: 60).

The really utopian element of *Blueprint for Survival* is its assertion that such a society could also 'give the fullest possible satisfaction to its members' (*The Ecologist* 1973: 320).

Blueprint linked human flourishing and social development to the de-industrialization of society rather than to economic expansion and material possessions, to

> [a] society made up of decentralized, self-sufficient communities, in which people work near their homes, have the responsibility of governing themselves, of running their schools, hospitals and welfare services. (*The Ecologist* 1973: 78)

Decentralization was at the heart of the better society. A less urban, less densely populated geographical and social structure would force people to rely on and take responsibility for local food production systems. At the same time, it would enable local autonomy and decision-making. Smaller societies, they argued, would enable people to develop rich and satisfying relationships with others, rather than being atomized individuals within an alienated mass society (*The Ecologist* 1973: 63–4). The ideal of self-sufficient but interrelated communities offered the best option for both ecological sustainability and social welfare.

Despite its insistence that a better society must be built on population reduction, and although the word 'survival' appears in the title, *The Ecologist*'s *Blueprint* did not suggest authoritarian solutions, but described local and participatory forms of democracy. But while its economic proposals were radical, its vision of sustainability was socially conservative. Referring to reductive functionalist sociological models, the writers saw any form of 'deviance' from social norms (illegitimacy, alcoholism) as indications of a disintegrating social system that could be cured by strengthening the nuclear family and small, inward-looking communities (*The Ecologist* 1973: 119). They did not question traditional gender roles or consider the cultural and political consequences of proposals to limit travel and migration. *Blueprint* was limited in another way, too, as its title suggests. As a formal utopian vision it feels rigid, thin and unappealing. The tone is descriptive and didactic. Its ideals for a sustainable society were expressed in the form of limited sketches of a few economic and structural principles with little apparent interest in imagining or exploring alternative lifestyles, identities or experiences.

Both the *Blueprint* and *The Limits to Growth* looked back to the nineteenth century to find inspiration for a vision of a better, more sustainable society. Both texts use the same short quote from John Stuart Mill:

> It is scarcely necessary to remark that a stationary condition of capital and population implies no stationary state of human improvement. There would be as much scope as ever for all kinds of mental culture, and moral and social progress; as much room for improving the Art of Living and much more likelihood of its being improved, when minds ceased to be engrossed by the art of getting on. (*Principles of Political Economy* [1857] quoted in Meadows et al. 1972: 175, and The Ecologist 1973: 79–80)

Blueprint, *Limits* and *Small is Beautiful* form a dense intertextual group. They refer mainly to each other and to a small handful of additional early environmentalist texts: Daly on the steady-state economy (1973); Ehrlich (1971) on exponential population growth; Commoner's *The Closing Circle* and its four 'laws' of ecology (1971); Dubos on 'the care and maintenance of a small planet' (Dubos and Ward 1972). Schumacher reaches wider to encompass Gandhi and Buddhist philosophy, but it is notable that none draw on Romantic traditions of nature philosophy, art or popular culture, and all three show a rather limited imagination of the social and cultural possibilities after growth. All three texts were also perhaps trapped by their own commitments to rational, statistical arguments. Referring frequently to current population and resource trends, to data sets and computer models, they suggest, even against their own explicit commitments to a change of culture, that a purely rational solution could be found to the limits to growth. I argue that the limits texts did not manage to paint attractive pictures of a stable-state economy. Their future visions were intellectually stimulating but limited in their appeal to the speculative and social imagination.

Nonetheless, the limits discourse introduced a novel set of ideas into environmental thought that profoundly shaped the conditions of green utopianism in the late twentieth century. The limits discourse has been criticized for relying on inaccurate data and reductive systems modelling. It is based on problematic assumptions about population growth. It lent credence to authoritarian solutions to environmental and social problems. But as we have seen, the apocalyptic logic of limits environmentalism opened up a new conceptual space in which human well-being could be separated from consumption and economic expansion. It suggested the possibility of major cultural and social structural shifts in the name of environmental sustainability. It demonstrated also that while data projections can help us to see where current economic paths are leading, they cannot produce ideas to live by. Imagining alternatives to industrial capitalism demands metaphysical renewal, not just an enlightened rationality, good management and incremental policy solutions. We will see how these utopian strands of the limits discourse led to more radically emancipatory ecocentric approaches in the next chapter. Below I move on to look at how the crisis logics of limits gave way, by the mid-1980s, to a more pragmatic and hopeful but perhaps less critical and imaginative discourse.

Sustainable development: paths to a liveable future

In 1984, the United Nations General Assembly mandated a new inquiry into the prospects for global development at a time of 'unprecedented growth in pressures on the human environment, with grave predictions about the human future becoming commonplace' (WCED 1987: 365). In 1987, the World Commission on Environment and Development (WCED) chaired by Gro Harlem Brundtland gave its report, *Our Common Future*. It set out a new diagnosis of global environment and development issues in the late twentieth century. In contrast to the 'world system' models favoured in the limits discourse, the sustainable development approach identified very different environmental problematics facing different parts of the globe. In developed Western economies, unsustainability meant that economic progress and prosperity caused the depletion of finite resources and the production of large-scale environmental problems. In less developed parts of the world, there was a direct link between poverty and overexploitation of local resources to meet basic needs, resulting in cycles of environmental decline and downward pressures on *per capita* income. The solution to both was a new ethical framework to guide the emergence of a more environmentally secure and a more economically equitable society. Sustainable forms of development would 'integrate production with resource conservation and enhancement... link[ing] both to the provision for all of an adequate livelihood base and equitable access to resources' (WCED 1987: 39–40).

The concept of sustainable development is about the hopeful prospect of an environmentally secure future in which human needs and aspirations can be fulfilled without undermining ecological systems (WCED 1987: 43). Its focus on the future is firmly present in the widely circulated Brundtland definition of sustainable development as 'development that meets the needs of the present without compromising the ability of future generations to meet their own needs' (WCED 1987: 43). Unlike in the limits discourse, however, the solution to the environmental problematic and the possibility for positive social change was not the end of economic growth, but the promotion of more and better growth, supported by new forms of technology, capitalist development and integrated governance (WCED 1987: 8). If economic growth can incorporate a new sensitivity to the finitude of the resource base and the importance of clean production, it can generate new material resources to support further rounds of sustainable development. From the mid-1980s onwards, the logic of sustainable development became dominant in environmental policy discourse and increasingly penetrated the popular environmental imagination (Glasbergen and Blowers 1995; Irwin 2001; Baker 2006; Elliott 2012; Blewitt 2014).

The journey from the limits to growth to sustainable development represents a major discursive shift. The narratives, metaphors and assumptions of the environmental problematic change. But it also reflects increasing institutionalization in the period after the limits discourse made a new public space for environmental crisis and concerns. The United Nations Environment Programme (UNEP) was founded in 1972 to embed environmental advocacy within the United Nations system.[7] The US Environmental Protection Agency (EPA) had been formed in 1970, around the same time as environmental departments in the UK and other European national governments. Regional and then national green political parties emerged, first in Australia and New Zealand in the early 1970s and then across Europe, some gaining power in coalition governments in the 1980s. By the mid-1980s, Greenpeace and Friends of the Earth were established as environmental NGOs. A succession of UN and UN-endorsed environmental reports gained attention through the 1970s into the 1980s: the UNEP Brandt Report in 1980, the *World Conservation Strategy* report, also 1980, and in the US the *Global 2000* report, 1980, commissioned by President Carter, identifying urgent environmental and resource problems. Environmental concerns, then, were increasingly articulated in the context of global political institutions, UN policy and international NGOs.

As sustainable development became a dominant storyline for environmental concern, the limits paradigm became less important. The discourse of sustainable development both relied upon and transformed the notion of physical limits to economic growth. Both take as their object the future relationship between ecological systems and socio-economic development on a planetary scale. Both seek to translate the ontological relationships they identify into linkages between economics and ecology at the social and political levels, especially in promoting an integrated governmental approach. The environmental sense of the adjective 'sustainable' was first developed within limits texts. Used interchangeably with terms like 'stable' and 'secure', it meant the capacity of something to endure or keep going continuously. Towards the end of *The Limits to Growth*, the noun "sustainability" is used to refer more explicitly to a goal or preference for a social system, signifying a state of global equilibrium 'built to last for generations' (Meadows et al. 1972: 158, 188). Similarly, *Blueprint* envisaged a 'stable' society that could be 'sustained indefinitely' (*The Ecologist* 1973: 34).

In the Brundtland Report it is development itself that is to be made sustainable. This shifts environmental discourse away from the idea that there are absolute ecological limits to growth. The Brundtland discourse of sustainable development envisages a future that is fundamentally continuous with the present. Development can be modestly reshaped. Societies can be set on reformist paths to a future in which economic growth supports rather than undermines ecological systems. The limits discourse recognized that the world systems they tried to map and predict contained stark differences of economic wealth and industrial development between nations. Indeed, key authors were anxious to hold the developed nations of the north responsible for associating development *per se* with economic expansion, and with importing ideologies of materialism and mass scale around the world (Schumacher 1993 [1973]). Many environmentalists actively (if not always successfully) tried to avoid neo-colonialist solutions (*The Ecologist* 1973) and acknowledged that some nations would have to continue to develop for longer than others. But eventually, the limits model insisted, growth must stop for the benefit of people and planet.

The Brundtland Report, by contrast, rejected the idea there was a single, systemic environmental crisis caused by economic growth in a finite system. Instead, it identified a series of 'thresholds' beyond which different ecosystems would become endangered (WCED 1987: 32–3). Limits worked with aggregated models using overall world trends in pollution, technological development, resource use and so on. Brundtland suggested that limits to growth are multiple, staggered and social rather than singular, absolute and physical. This is not to say that the Brundtland Report did not address environmental degradation and resource challenge. It examined problems of population growth, food shortages and energy supply. It looked at industrial and urban pollution. It explored biodiversity, species loss, rainforest depletions and global waste disposal. It spelt out the pressures on global commons, from the oceans and Antarctica to space. It paid special attention to people in developing countries facing life-threatening challenges of desertification, deforestation, pollution and poverty. But its storyline for the environmental problematic disaggregated limits and rejected the threat of overshoot and collapse. Brundtland argued that

[g]rowth has no set limit in terms of population or resource use beyond which lies ecological disaster. Different limits hold for the use of energy, materials, water and land. (WCED 1987: 45)

Brundtland said that a sudden and catastrophic loss of the resource base was far less likely than slow environmental decline in specific geographic areas or environmental systems. While the limits model looked towards a temporal break that would be encountered sometime in the twenty-first century, *Our Common Future* broke the environmental future down into smaller steps. It referred to the needs of successive future generations, replacing a single apocalyptic horizon with a plural and shifting one. In response to the complex environmental and development crises facing the world in the late twentieth century, sustainable development recouped a liveable future, referring to 'development paths' that would lead from dirty, depleting economic growth to a future of clean growth that conserved the resource base (WCED 1987: 309). There was no need for a dramatic change in social practices or economic systems. More economic growth was needed to ensure that basic needs could be met and to secure greener and more sustainable trade and technology.

Sustainable development, then, expressed dissatisfaction with the state of the environment and offered optimistic hope for a better future. It articulated a commitment that 'the future should be a better, healthier place than the present and the past' (Blewitt 2014: 32). But its solutions were moderate, reformist, practical and administrative rather than radical and idealist. Brundtland launched many policy programmes for national and regional reform. The best-known example was Agenda 21, the outcome of the UN Conference on Environment and Development held in Rio de Janeiro in 1992. Agenda 21 marked the moment at which sustainable development became the goal of policy-makers. It sought to map out the paths to 'a safer, more prosperous future' for all and to ensuring 'better protected and managed ecosystems' (UNCED 1993: 3). This meant a more free and dynamic trade system and enhanced integration of environmental issues into economic decision-making at all levels of government. As sustainable development moved towards implementation, it reproduced existing socio-economic structures and values and made economic growth the single most important solution to environmental problems. According to Agenda 21, developing nations would benefit from unfettered global markets, heightened competition and less national protectionism (UNCED

1993: 4). Richer nations could accommodate environmental issues into policy-making by attributing economic value to environmental goods.

The moral, political and cultural engagements with the future that had been so visible in earlier environmentalism began to disappear in Agenda 21. Although still linked to visions of a better future, sustainability discourse dilutes the transformative utopianism connected with limits to growth. Logics of efficiency dominated national and international environmental planning, calls for more data and integrated global management to shift the world onto sustainable development paths (see, for example, UNCED 1993: 12–13). Environmental issues and their solutions were framed less as matters of politics, values and culture, and more in terms of prevailing (and increasingly neoliberal) market rationalities and technocratic management. Agenda 21 did have a more local dimension that brought back in the promise of more ethical and utopian strands. Brundtland had argued that sustainable development must have a democratic mandate: local participation and community knowledge were crucial to real sustainable development. It urged local authorities to promote citizens' initiatives and devolve power so that communities might pursue diverse, grass-roots visions of sustainability (WCED 1987: 63).

Throughout the 1990s the challenge of Local Agenda 21 was (partially) taken up by local governments, NGOs and environmental campaigners.[8] It was estimated that 300 local authorities had developed sustainability action plans by 1995, with processes for implementation underway in twenty-nine countries (Whittaker 1995: 20; Blewitt 2014: 12). Local visions for sustainability proliferated and communities explored what sustainability would mean for them – from schemes to improve public transport in Leicester, UK (Roberts 2000) to calls for participatory council budgeting and the provision of sophisticated recycling schemes in Porto Alegre, Brazil (Menegat 2002). But Local Agenda 21 quickly became colonized by instrumental and pragmatic politics. Local visions were constrained by limited resources and local leaders too often preferred to guide and inform publics about what sustainable development should be rather than facilitate two-way engagements. At the local level too, the distinctively environmental aspects of sustainability often disappeared into a complex mix of economic, community and quality-of-life concerns.

By the mid-1990s, many commentators were arguing that sustainable development had become essentially a programme for 'inventing new institutional structures for managing the environment' (Redclift 1996: 1; see also Springett and Redclift 2015). The emphasis on implementing sustainable development privileged the doable elements of environmental solutions and saw the way forward as a matter of incremental linear steps. The 'immaterial, the unquantifiable and the unpredictable' elements of the environmental problematic were largely effaced from public and policy debates (Szerszynski et al. 1996: 9; Imran et al. 2014). If limits functioned as a site of contestation over global issues of environmental futures and an opportunity to examine the goals or ends of economic development, sustainable development closed down around the means. There is little ethical and no utopian engagement with what might be a better future. Sachs suggests that dominant sustainable development discourse conceived of it in terms of 'efficiency', focusing on the 'rational planning of planetary conditions' (1999: 84; see also Kambites 2014). Sustainability becomes the province of experts and policy-makers. Questions of 'sufficiency', attention to metaphysical questions of the human good life and the possibility of change, are excluded (Sachs 1999: 84; Springett and Redclift 2015).

From limits to sustainability

The story I have told here of course simplifies developments in environmental discourse in the late twentieth century. Sustainable development cannot be reduced to the technocratic and progressive version that dominated in global policy-making. Activists and more radical environmental voices mobilized around the idea, using it to explore politically and philosophically radical visions of environmental and social futures and to press for democratic, humane and above all urgent change to protect vulnerable people as well as vulnerable environments (Blewitt 2014; Imran et al. 2014). Indeed, sustainability has always functioned in environmental discourse as a notoriously vague, broad or contested concept. Sustainability is hard to disagree with and easy to claim for a wide range of policies, positions and actions (Torgerson 1995; Yearley 1996). It is also true that the limits discourse did not simply disappear from environmental debates after the 1980s. It continues to inform radical ecopolitical visions and arguments. Its main authors have continued to measure globally aggregated figures in updated world systems models (see, for example, Meadows et al. 1992, 2004). Annual updates on the relationship between the global economy and biospheric support systems inspired by the Club of Rome are produced by Lester Brown's Worldwatch Institute (www.worldwatch.org). In recent years, economists and others have suggested that the Club of Rome's statistical predictions were broadly correct (Turner 2008; Bardi 2011; Giddens 2011) and re-asserted the possibility of no-growth environmental economics (Jackson 2009; Zovanyi 2012).

Nonetheless, within twenty years of the emergence of a radical and critical environmentalism in the 1970s, the popular and policy mainstream was dominated by a progressive, conservative and technocratic discourse. Sustainable development continues to dominate mainstream policy and political frameworks for thinking about environmental futures (Baker 2006; Elliott 2012; Blewitt 2014; Sachs 2015). In recent years it has become even more wedded to neoliberal market solutions and technocratic management. Reflecting on the outcomes of Rio+20, held in 2012 to take stock of two decades of UN environmental policy commitments, Blewitt notes that the hopeful progressive mode that characterized sustainable development in its early years had become 'hesitant, modest and accommodationist' (2014: 14; see also Imran et al. 2014). The sustainable development agenda becomes more pragmatic, less transformative. It takes up much of the public political and cultural space available for thinking about environmental futures, leaving less room for the critical, creative play of the utopian imagination, for radical alternatives and unsettling proposals.

Sustainable development is related to and part of discourses of ecological modernization that have been at work since the late twentieth century (Hajer 1995, 1996). Proponents of the ecological modernization thesis suggest that it names real material, technological and institutional processes by which Western societies are reflexively adjusting to environmental problems and critiques in an orderly and progressive fashion (Spaargaren et al. 2000; Mol and Jänicke 2009; Mol et al. 2009). They argue that the institutions, ideologies and cultural ensembles that environmentalism held responsible for the systemic causes of environmental crisis can be reformed. Societies can progress from an era of growth that has been dirty, damaging and nearly self-defeating to a new era that is clean, ecologically cautious, and sustainable. Others, however, argue that ecological modernization is better understood as a form of cultural politics (Hajer 1996) in which the *idea* that environmental problems can be resolved without radical cultural, political or economic change reshapes the discursive landscape. My argument in this chapter has been that as ecological modernization has taken hold in Western cultures, politics and policy-making, it has left less space for green utopias that envisage radically different ways of living. As environmentalism was taken up by the institutions of the modernist mainstream, so its ideals and utopian hopes were modified to fit an overwhelming commitment to economic growth.

However problematic, conservative and sometimes uninspiring, however unrealistic and unrealizable, the visions and arguments of the limits discourse introduced new ethical and metaphysical engagements with alternative green futures. They expressed utopian desires for something radically other than modified late capitalism. The way out of environmental crisis could not simply be a rational administrative decision to follow a sustainable development path. Rather, it involved self-reflection and self-examination in Western cultures. It involved a critical analysis of the necessity of unlimited material expansion and a philosophical call to ask searching questions about how much is enough. It suggested that human well-being might be pursued via different structures, lifestyles and values. Limits asked whether a more sustainable and less ecologically damaging economy could also generate new prospects for human security and happiness. It challenged the taken-for-granted notions that growth would make things better. An explicit focus on the utopian dimensions of this discourse enables us to trace the visions that it made available, and what is lost when environmentalism adopts more reformist and mainstream positions.

I have analysed limits and sustainability in this chapter because they successively shaped the mainstream of environmental concerns. They also shared a rather distanced account of the environmental predicament in terms of interlocking global systems. The limits paradigm often used the metaphor of spaceship earth to convey the finite natural resources and the integrated ecosystems of the planet. The Brundtland Report likewise constructed its claims with reference to the earth as a unified object, a 'fragile ball' floating in space, the emblem of a seamless and singular global biosphere (WCED 1987: 1). Drawing on the whole planet image, the limits discourse suggested that economics must become subservient to ecology. Ecology tells us the real truths about planetary life-processes; economics must become the science that tells us how much resource there is and how to cautiously conserve it. Sustainable development discourse likewise suggests that the disciplines and practices of economics and environmental management should be closely integrated – but this time, environmental concerns are to be added to economic decision-making. The logic of both is to treat the earth as a single system and to pitch hopes for the future at the scale of planetary structures. Both discourses lack a situated perspective and a bottom-up future vision. The next chapter looks at utopian proposals for a sustainable society that start with the personal, the experiential, the metaphysical and the local.

3
Deep Ecology: Wild Nature, Radical Visions

Crisis, culture and consciousness

We saw in the previous chapter that environmentalism can open up challenges to mainstream values and authorize utopian attempts to articulate social alternatives. We also saw that as the narrative of sustainable development came to dominate the public and policy sphere, mainstream green hopes became more modest and reformist. This chapter examines a body of thought in which the utopian challenge of early environmentalism was developed in a radically new direction. Already in the early 1970s, thinkers such as Arne Naess (1973) were distinguishing between two kinds of environmentalism. Naess argued that there was a shallow ecology movement which saw the environmental problematic in terms of managing resource and pollution issues through institutional reform, regulating bad practices and developing new technologies. He contrasted this with deep ecology, which saw environmental crisis as the inevitable outcome of the instrumental, technocentric values of Western modernity, and called for a transformative greening of consciousness and culture. As the two strands diverged through the 1970s and 1980s, deep ecology explored ever more critical and creative utopian alternatives to Western culture and lifestyles. This chapter explores the tenets of this ecological philosophy and the debates in ecological politics that animated radical environmentalism and shaped green future thinking, locating a deep well of utopianism in radical ecophilosophy.

Deep ecology calls for a fundamental break with the dominant humanist traditions of Western philosophy and culture since the Enlightenment. Instead of seeing humans as separate from nature (because of their consciousness, rationality, evolutionary superiority or eternal souls), deep ecology insists that 'there is no firm ontological divide in the field of existence' (Fox 1990a: 194). Humans are part of the natural world, and nature is part of us. Drawing on this holistic or monist ontology, deep ecology adopts a strong ethical norm of ecocentric equality. It argues that, like humans, all organic entities have the right to what Naess (1989) calls self-realization – the capacity to unfold or blossom in their own way. Deep ecology values things first and foremost for themselves, not for their instrumental or use-value to human beings. In ecocentric (nature-centred) approaches to ethics, organisms and ecosystems become objects of moral consideration and fair treatment in their own right and as part of a wider respect for the intrinsic value of nature.[1] Deep ecologists, then, propose an alternative to contemporary anthropocentric (human-centred) ways of thinking and to the human domination and exploitation of the natural world. They argue that environmental crisis demands a fundamental transformation of human consciousness, culture and socio-economic systems. Their entire approach is driven by utopian desire, and deep ecology has also produced a rich and lively stream of detailed utopian visions for a greener society.

Deep ecology emerged in the same time-frame as limits environmentalism and the two overlapped extensively in the early 1970s. Texts like *The Limits to Growth* (Meadows et al. 1972), *Small is Beautiful* (Schumacher 1993 [1973]) and *Blueprint for Survival* (*The Ecologist* 1973) were critical of Western industrial societies and what they took to be their dominant values. They briefly sketched social systems and lifestyles that would avert environmental catastrophe and were hopeful that these alternatives would also enhance human welfare and satisfaction. But the main assumptions of the limits discourse were shallow, in Naess's terms. They focused on the problems that finite natural resources and growing environmental pollution were causing for humans. They presented a new image of humanity as dependent on a finite and even a fragile planet – but they didn't see humans as *part of* the planet. They emphasized systemic links between economic and ecological spheres, not intimate connections between person and planet (Roszak 1979). Limits discourse was framed in rational and economistic terms. It sought to influence policy-makers through what Naess calls 'threats' and 'predictions' (1973: 99), as in the Club of Rome's model. The discourse of deep ecology would be framed instead in terms of values, feeling and subjectivity. It sought not top-down policy changes but transformations of culture, consciousness and politics.

Rather than systems and numbers, then, deep ecology focused on the ecological norms, values and ethics that would underpin a better way of living with nature. It explored ontological questions about the nature of reality, examined epistemological issues of how we understand the natural world, and presented ethical challenges about how we should relate to it. Deep ecology proposed that changes in culture and consciousness could protect nature, enhance human well-being and extend the sphere of emancipated being. To develop these arguments, deep ecology drew on a different set of texts and intellectual traditions than the limits discourse.[2] It drew on scientific ecology's observations about the interconnectedness of all organisms, and its non-reductionist celebration of the diversity and complexity of life. It was also linked to grass-roots environmentalist politics. Deep ecology made use of insights from Eastern spiritual and philosophical traditions that emphasized holistic ontologies and explored ways of effacing the ego and the individual self. Some deep ecologists located elements of an ecocentric approach in radical readings of Christian theology (Naess 1989). Others embraced Romantic and transcendentalist literary and philosophical traditions that emphasized the human spiritual and aesthetic need for wild nature (Devall and Sessions 1985). They drew on what in the 1970s was becoming known as the new physics, the quantum and other post-Newtonian approaches that were revealing the limits of mechanistic and atomistic conceptions of the physical universe and questioning linear models of causality, suggesting a physical world composed of interrelated matter in dynamic flux rather than discrete and stable objects.

Many deep ecologists pointed to Descartes and early natural philosophy as the moment at which human consciousness was decisively separated from the world it observed (Sale 1985; Naess 1989). Others suggested that as humans became more enmeshed in the industrial urban societies they had created, they became more instrumental, losing touch with nature and with broader conceptions of life and value. It is unsurprising, then, that some deep ecological thinking looked positively at pre-modern and non-Western cultures as sources of alternative ways of living and being. But these were not straightforwardly nostalgic or conservative visions (Garforth 2005). They were, as Frankel (1987) and Kumar (1987) insisted at the time, self-consciously *post-industrial*. They saw themselves as part of a paradigm shift, moving away from modern rationalities, realist ontologies and scientific epistemologies and towards a new way of being in the world. This was not to be a reversion to the past, but rather a break with modernity informed by countercultural politics. Deep ecology, especially in Naess's vision (and in the social ecology of Bookchin, discussed below) combined an ecocentric orientation with commitments to social justice and a critique of hierarchy. Deep ecology is also infused with the politics of emancipation and personal liberation, a focus on the possibility for self-development and consciousness raising that marked the new left and feminism in the West in the 1960s and 1970s.

Combining radical new ideas about the intrinsic value of nature with these egalitarian and liberatory impulses, deep ecology expresses a desire for nothing less than the complete transformation of modern social structures and lifestyles. It articulates a nature metaphysics that opens up new modes of envisioning green futures. It is not necessarily a hopeful discourse, in the sense of looking forward positively in the expectation of immediate change.[3] Nor is it progressive in a linear sense – indeed, it is premised on the rejection of Western ideas of progress and the need for a fundamental break with the status quo. Its utopianism lies rather in a critical and exploratory orientation towards different ways of living and being and a deeply emancipatory politics (Eck-ersley 1992: 18). Influential strands of deep ecology aimed to develop a new kind of consciousness that would begin with a felt understanding of human embeddedness in the natural world. Acting on this consciousness would not simply protect and preserve natural resources, but would allow all life to flourish and unfold in its own way. Personal growth and individual happiness emerge not from having more and maximizing material welfare but from having less and maxi-mizing opportunities to connect with others.

In this chapter I examine the utopianism of radical strands of ecological philosophy. I start by exploring the metaphysi-cal and ethical tenets of deep ecology, moving on to consider the social and political proposals for sustainability that it implies. Firstly, then, I focus on the utopian*ism* of deep green philosophy, characterized by open-ended, expressive desires for another way of being. The texts produced by deep eco-logical philosophers in the 1970s and 1980s are infused with utopian yearning. They powerfully express the sense that the lack of embeddedness in nature in modern societies damages and alienates human beings as well as environments. They vividly elaborate alternative models of consciousness and subjectivity, values and ethics that would enable humans to live better with other life-forms and are rooted in an ethic of care for and connectedness with nature which offers new forms of satisfaction. I begin with Naess's proposals for a deep ecosophy (1973, 1989) and then explore how Devall and Sessions (1985) developed these ideas into claims for ecocentric equality linked to the value of wilderness. I draw extensively on Eckersley's (1992) account of the emancipa-tory turn in ecological thought in the late 1970s and early 1980s and its generation of novel ways of understanding, supporting and developing human autonomy and growth in step with the natural world.

Secondly, I look at some of the more formal utopian pro-posals for an alternative society that emerged from deep green philosophy. Deep ecology rejects modern Western attitudes and values, its social structures and systems. Its radically emancipatory programme involved visions of other modes of life: politically decentralized and locally embedded, economi-cally modest and ecologically cautious, attuned to nonhuman temporalities and cycles rather than separate from the natural world. Deep ecology holds that new forms of ecological consciousness and environmental ethics grow best in communities that are small, self-sufficient, stable and autonomous. I look at three of the most prominent proposals for new forms of ecological settlement that emerged in the 1980s. Animating many discussions of deep ecology's social proposals is the bioregionalist vision suggested by Berg and Dasmann's (1977) 'Reinhabiting California' (see also Berg 2002) and developed by Sale into proposals for living-in-place in *Dwellers in the Land* (1985). Preceding Naess's articulation of a deep ecology, Bookchin had been exploring proposals for *Remaking Society* (1989) along eco-anarchist lines since the late 1960s.

Deep green philosophy and utopian desire

It is hard to imagine a more fundamental challenge to the socio-economic structures and lifestyles of late capitalism than that which came from deep ecologists in the 1980s. Like advocates of the limits to growth thesis, they argued that Western societies must fundamentally rethink systems of production and consumption and move away from large-scale agriculture and industrial technology. They must reject the expansionist models that tie social progress to increasing economic growth and resist the superficial pleasures of commodity consumption. But they also suggested that we needed to remake our consciousness, learn to see ourselves anew as physically, sensuously, psychologically and spiritually connected to nonhuman nature. We needed a new conception of what it means to grow and develop as a human being. We needed to develop an ethos that would respect the right of all earthly things to develop and flourish. As individuals, we should swap shopping sprees for thinking like a tree, stop competing to own more and start becoming richer in our connections to others and to nature. As communities, we should pursue self-determination and self-sufficiency rather than being passive cogs in national and global systems dedicated to economic expansion. In a phrase usually attributed to Naess, we should adopt ways of life that are simple in means and rich in ends (see also Devall 1988).

This vision of a less materialistic, more contemplative way of life has tended, in caricatures of the green movement, to be portrayed as self-denying, austere, joyless, a hair shirt philosophy and a politics of sacrifice. But deep ecologists have consistently presented their desire for an alternative to Western models in terms of freedom, well-being, even joy (Naess 1989). An ecocentric world represents freedom from the modern world of competition, consumption and alienation (Roszak 1979). A less materially rich world would offer new freedom to pursue satisfactions through 'love, play, creative expression...intimate human relationships and spiritual growth' (Devall and Sessions 1985: 68). It would open up new ways of connecting with nature. Radically ecocentric approaches emerging through the 1970s into the 1980s saw environmental crisis, then, as the opportunity for 'metaphysical reconstruction' and spiritual and moral development (Eckersley 1992: 19), the opportunity for 'a fresh inquiry into the meaning of the good life' (Sachs 1999: 186). As Naess put it:

> [environmental] crisis...could contribute to open our minds to sources of meaningful life which have largely gone unnoticed or been depreciated in our efforts to adapt to the urbanized, techno-industrial mega society. (1989: 24)

Naess's deep ecosophy,[4] outlined in his book *Ecology, Community and Lifestyle*, insists that nothing short of a new ontology is needed to save nature and save humans. The new ecocentric cultures and ways of life needed to move beyond environmental crisis must be rooted in a rearrangement of reality itself. He proposes a new metaphysics that recognizes not separate entities with essential properties, but interconnection. All things are constituted in their relationships with others. Drawing on the philosophy of Spinoza, Naess adopted a monist ontology in which 'everything flows' (1989: 50) and organisms are temporary 'knots in the biospherical net or field of intrinsic relations' (1973: 95). Naess argued that Enlightenment thinking took a wrong turn when it separated humanity from this dense and lively world, adopting instead a mechanistic, atomistic and empiricist framework for understanding nature. Deep ecology rejects these modern 'man-in-Environment' images and adopts instead a 'relational, total-field' (1973: 95) approach. For Naess, deep ecology is a philosophy, not a pragmatic programme for environmental action or a scientific or political platform. It draws from scientific ecology's apprehension of nature in terms of interconnections and the relationship between parts and wholes, but aims to link these insights to wider questions of metaphysics, ethics and the human good life. It is dedicated to change in the name of environmental improvement, but locates the source of political change in individual experience, culture and consciousness.

Here environmental ethics is not an external code of conduct to be imposed on individuals. It comes from a new experiential grasp of the world and our place within it. Really caring for nature involves a metaphysical shift: '[o]ne's ethics in environmental questions are based largely on how one sees reality' (1989: 67). If all things are interconnected, then self-realization – growth, development, flourishing of an entity or system – is not separate from or at the expense of others but instead depends on relationships (1989: 85). If all things are part of the same processes of life and growth, then all parts of the natural world have, in principle, the same right to self-realization. Environmental ethics is not a matter of following moral axioms or ethical prescriptions. An eco-centric egalitarian ethos does not emerge purely from logic. It is a phenomenological matter, derived from experience and empathy, rooted in feelings about and developed within the wider world. Naess cites Kant's distinction between the 'beautiful' and the 'moral' action (1989: 85). Deep ecology prefers an ethics in which a 'person acts beautifully when acting benevolently from inclination', orienting to nature as 'something valuable which we are inclined to treat with joy and respect' (Naess 1989: 85). It rejects the 'moral action' that is motivated purely by an external law. In the latter model, Naess argues, nature becomes 'something strange or hostile' towards which we must act well *against* our feelings. Humans are embedded in the natural world, existing together in a 'relational field' (1989: 55) that links objects and experiences together and binds the self into the wider world. Becoming aware of these relations will enable people to perceive the value and diversity of nonhuman life through a combination of observation, sensual experience, identification and rational reflection.

The norms of deep ecology, then, are for many theorists intuitive or 'experiential' rather than purely intellectual or rational (Devall and Sessions 1985: 69). An ethics of nature is rooted in the erosion or blurring of boundaries between human and nonhuman, between inside and outside, between self and other (Sargisson 2000). Environmental care is an extension of human responsibility for the self. Observing that 'there is no completely isolatable I', Naess invokes the idea of a 'deep, comprehensive ecological self' (1989: 164, 176). Devall and Sessions use the term 'self-in-Self' to refer to a similar idea – that humans can grow and develop by relinquishing the narrow selfish ego and opening out to encounters and relationships with others, including nonhuman nature (1985: 67). We mature and flourish by making identifications and becoming part of a wider 'organic wholeness'. And 'if we hurt the rest of Nature we are harming ourselves' (1985: 67–8). For Devall and Sessions, the cultivation of an ecological consciousness is at the heart of deep ecology. Humans must develop new forms of attentiveness to nonhuman others and cultures which respect the rights of all things to self-realization: 'no one is saved unless we are all saved' (1985: 7).

Devall and Sessions contribute a distinctive element to deep ecology by arguing that wilderness is crucial to this new environmental consciousness and ethics.[5] Wilderness is a 'landscape or ecosystem that has been minimally disrupted by the intervention of humans' (Devall and Sessions 1985: 110). For many deep ecologists, it is a most vivid and powerful source of ecocentric values. They argue that wilderness can never be reduced to utilitarian calculations of its value to humans. It always exceeds us. Wilderness challenges us to respect an ecocentric ethic that emphasizes the intrinsic value of nonhuman entities and ecosystems and their right to flourish. Wilderness is also a crucial site where individuals can cultivate a new consciousness. Devall and Sessions draw on the nature writing of US preservationist and founder of the national parks movement John Muir, who wrote that 'wilderness is unity and interrelation, is alive and familiar...the very stones are talkative, sympathetic, brotherly' (in Devall and Sessions 1985: 110). The direct experience of untrammelled, uncultivated wild spaces enables humans to 'appreciate non-human self', to understand that 'mountains and rivers are [self-]actualizing' (Devall and Sessions 1985: 112), and to feel the importance of adopting a modest and humble attitude in relation to nature.

In parallel with Devall and Sessions, Fox developed a 'transpersonal' approach to deep ecology, an 'experiential invitation' to ecocentric ethics (Fox 1990b: 49). In this approach, the cultivation of an expansive, outward-looking, relational sense of self is at the heart of environmental care. If we can identify with other beings and interrelated systems as, like ourselves, self-realizing, unfolding and growing, then ecological ethics will follow. For Fox, this is a psychological, not a rational or logical, connection (Fox 1990a; Eckersley 1992: 63). Similar arguments have been developed by feminist philosophers, locating the best possibilities for an embodied or experiential ethics in the relationship between women and nature. Contemporary ecofeminist voices argue that this relationship is not one of essential (biological) similarities or intuitive, empathetic connections, but rather emerges from a shared history and 'logic of domination' in which women and nature are treated as inferior, irrational others (Eckersley 1992: 64; see also Warren 1996).[6] In these iterations, ecofeminism links ecocentric thought to a wider set of emancipatory political philosophies critical of modernist binaries. It opens out to post-structuralist and even posthumanist analyses of domination (Merchant 1982, 2003; Haraway 1991; Plumwood 1993, 2001; Braidotti 2013). Plumwood's work has been particularly important in linking the domination and exploitation of women and nature to a dominant modern 'cult of rationality' (2001: 5) that instrumentally treats the material and ecological world as worthless, renewable and dispensable.

What links these approaches is an ecocentric ethic or an idea of biocentric egalitarianism. Attributing equal worth to nonhuman beings, suggesting they are not ultimately different in kind to humans, presents a severe challenge to Enlightenment humanism. Attributing value on the basis of interconnection and system, not on the basis of an individual entity, is even more challenging. Descartes cast the perceiving, knowing human subject as a rational mind separated from the material world (even to a certain extent from his own body). Ecocentric critics argue that this rationalist foundation for knowing the world marks the beginning of a fatal separation of humanity from the web of connections and relations of nature. It drew value into the sphere of human subjectivity and perception, treating the material world as having meaning and worth only in relation to human needs and desires. Many ecological philosophers argue that this attitude of human separateness is at the root of the environmental problematic. It founds a hierarchy of value with nature, instrumentalized, at the bottom. It legitimates the domination and exploitation of material resources and global ecosystems for human needs. In response, deep ecology presents a 'comprehensive religious and philosophical worldview' (Devall and Sessions 1985: 65) that expresses a deeply utopian desire for a complete alternative.

Deep ecology locates the source of socio-political change in the desiring subject. The only appropriate response to environmental crisis is to urge and imagine a radical transformation of culture and consciousness. This visionary and expressive utopianism separates deep ecology from other environmentalist discourses. Sustainable development approaches, as we have seen, emphasize continuities with existing values and structures and see the future in terms of incremental steps. Limits discourses argued for a break with current structures and practices, but their green futures started with the prospects for a rational reinvention of socio-economic systems. By rooting its model of change in the need for self-transformation and new metaphysical and spiritual paradigms, deep ecology (re-)connects environmentalism with Romantic and transcendentalist traditions. It changed the vocabulary through which green hopes were articulated. Rather than exploring specific environmental issues, criticizing contemporary economic systems, or proposing new social structures, it explores green desire in philosophical terms, speaking of and to matters of love, emancipation, being, nature and integrity. It imagines the 'deep pleasure and satisfaction we [might] receive from close partnerships with other forms of life' (Naess 1973: 96), rather than setting out abstract ethical imperatives.

Deep ecology makes green issues into personal concerns. It brings home the need for transformation, and locates the most important step in individual consciousness. It suggests that everyone can open their eyes to a new world, identify and express empathetic feelings for the nonhuman other, and act in accordance with these feelings. The personal, desiring and metaphysical character of deep ecology is, I suggest, its most utopian aspect. But this is not a practical utopianism, nor does it produce descriptive images of alternative futures. Its language of metaphysics and intuitive ethical commitments can feel removed from everyday life. Deep ecological discourse can often seem romantic and self-absorbed. It has much to say about a 'meditative dancing in the wonder of the cosmos' (Devall and Sessions 1985: 114), but less to say about who puts the recycling out or how different kinds of people might experience being in touch with nature. For some deep ecologists, pure nature, and wilderness in particular, take on a kind of mystical power over human agency, and lessons from nature are privileged over social choices. But there is a pragmatic and political dimension to deep ecological vision, not just a romantic and desiring utopianism, which we explore in the next section.

Ecopolitics and utopian visions

Since the 1970s, radically ecocentric thinkers have produced formal proposals for sustainable societies. As we have seen, for deep ecologists modern Western cultures are not only destroying global ecosystems but are also working against the cultivation of a more responsible and ultimately satisfying other-directed consciousness for human subjects. Materialist values have chased out spiritual and relational ones. Contemporary societies are infused with technocentric ideologies that promote efficient, scientific ways of doing things, neglecting both care for nature and human well-being. Economies are designed for the maximum use of natural resources through global markets and the profit motive. Industrial technologies enable large-scale exploitation of nature while at the same time alienating human workers from their creative labour.

Decision-making is located far away from the communities who must live with the consequences, and increasingly global forces of capital and power undermine the capacity to care for local environments. Lifestyles are dedicated to the superficial pleasures of consumption and standardized mass entertainment.

Ecocentric philosophy and politics offer an alternative to every aspect of contemporary Western societies and lifestyles. The core propositions of the deep green utopia are straightforward. Imagine living in a small community which is largely self-sufficient in food, fuel and shelter. Things are produced for need, not for growth and expansion, using small-scale technologies and renewable energy to conserve natural resources and limit environmental impact to a minimum. You know your local landscape intimately – the names of the trees, the nuances of climate, the current state of the nearest watershed – and have close relationships with neighbours. You rarely travel very far. Wherever possible, decisions are made at the lowest level and people play an active part in local politics. Hierarchical systems of power are limited; so are markets and commodity production. No-one has much, so material inequalities are fairly small; everyone has the right to flourish and blossom in their own way, so a liberal model of social justice should prevail. You have much, much less stuff and shopping is limited, and you work hard. But your work will be personally fulfilling and socially useful, and you may work for much less time than in contemporary societies. You will have more time and more opportunities for self-development through spiritual practices, education, arts, culture and personal relationships.

In a (rather reductive) nutshell, these are the basic structures and ways of life of deep ecology's political utopia. It proposes a sustainable society built on an ecocentric philosophy. The broad outlines of a radically green social and economic order are clearly evident in some of the founding texts of deep ecology. A vocabulary of simplicity, sufficiency and embeddedness circulates through key texts (Naess 1973, 1989; Devall and Sessions 1985; Sachs 1999). But the main philosophical thinkers in deep ecology tend to be rather sketchy about the practical arrangements for sustainable societies. Systematic proposals for deep green social structures, material foundations and political organization are found in more explicitly political expressions of the ecocentric approach. As the deep ecological position crystallized as a distinctive political ideology in the late 1970s and 1980s, ideas about the structures and practices of the good green society began to be articulated in more detail. As Dobson (1995) argues, it is precisely this distinctive vision of the good life that sets radical ecology apart from reformist environmentalism, indeed, that makes it a political ideology. This is not to say that there is a singular, unified deep green utopia; ecological politics is full of debate and dissent. But deep ecology's tenets of ecocentric equality and holistic ontology, its critique of the human and ecological consequences of a technocentric society, commit it to certain economic and political structures and cultural principles: limits to growth and steady-state economics, decentralized decision-making and living-in-place (Dobson 1995).

In terms of economic structures and a philosophy of small is beautiful, the green utopias of deep ecology have a good deal in common with those of the limits discourse. But ecocentric visions place much more emphasis on transformations of consciousness and culture than we have so far seen in environmental utopianism. Their proposals for a green society are predicated not solely on the need to conserve resources and avoid systemic catastrophe, but on the desire to expand the sphere of freedom and flourishing for both nature and humans (Eckersley 1992: 19). For deep ecologists, advocating a steady-state economy is secondary to exploring an ethos of 'sufficiency' (Sachs 1999: 185) – a conscious paring down of human needs and the substitution of cultural and spiritual for material pleasures. Deep ecology is also more committed to decentralized models of the green society than the limits discourse, which often implicitly retained the ideal of the nation state in its future projections.[7] For deep ecologists, the sustainable society must be made from the bottom up. Social structures must be appropriate to high levels of individual freedom of action and conscience, and any centralization of power is generally viewed with suspicion. Deep ecology's empathetic and intuitive approach to ethics is also important. Caring for nature depends on direct experience and first-hand knowledge of particular environments and places. There is therefore a strong pull towards localism and autonomy in deep green political philosophy.

One influential articulation of the social structures and lifestyle of deep ecology is the philosophy and politics of bioregionalism. These ideas first came to prominence in a short article by Berg and Dasmann setting out a powerful vision for 'reinhabiting California' (1977).[8] Bioregionalism is explicitly about taking the abstract philosophical tenets of deep ecology and translating them into a proactive and practical project for living with nature. Berg and Dasmann's polemical piece suggested that disruptive and dangerous rational-industrial civilizations had come to occupy or colonize the US and Europe. It was time to repair the land and (re-)learn how to live with the biotic community of a particular area. Bioregionalism argued that future societies must be founded on an ethos and practice of 'living-in-place': that is, 'following the necessities and pleasures of life as they are uniquely presented by a particular site' (Berg and Dasmann 1977: 399). Bioregionalism articulates both a material vision of self-sufficient and sustainable dwelling and an alternative culture and ethos of embeddedness which will enable the cultivation of a properly ecocentric consciousness and ethics:

> In a modern context based on the separation of society from the natural world, bioregionalists stress the importance of reinhabiting one's place and earthly home. A bioregion represents the intersection of vernacular culture, place-based behavior, and community. Bioregionalists believe that we should *return* to the place 'there is', the landscape itself, the place we inhabit and the communal region we depend on. (McGinnis 1999: 3)

In *Dwellers in the Land* (1985), Sale drew together a formal set of prescriptions for bioregionalism, describing the political, economic and social structures that would be needed for a decentralized, ecocentric future. Like Berg and Dasmann, Sale argued that scientific and industrial worldviews had led not only to imminent environmental catastrophe but also to a disenchantment of the world with debilitating consequences for the human psyche (1985: 20–2). Bioregionalism offered a politics of hope and a practical means for learning how to treat the earth with 'awe and admiration, respect and veneration' (Sale 1985: 42). At its heart is the cultivation of a sense of place. This idea refers both to detailed knowledge and understanding of a particular 'life-territory' – its topography, climate, resources and biota – and to a feeling for that place (Sale 1985: 50). The bioregion is where resource issues and environmental problems become real to people, 'where abstractions and intangibles give way to the here and now, the seen and felt, the real and known' (1985: 53). It is also the scale at which people can cultivate the capacity to identify with their local environment and rediscover pre-modern, pre-industrial folkways and knowledge.

Above all, the bioregional vision involves bringing the scale of social organization down to something much more modest than contemporary nation states and global economies, linking it to particular territories and ecosystems. Sale proposes a green alternative based on social settlements of 500–1,000 people, linked into communities of 5–10,000 members that would be able to produce the means of subsistence from their local area (Sale 1985: 64). These communities should be run on principles of conservation and sustainability, not economic growth. They would contain a good deal of internal complexity and interdependency. Land would be worked communally, not privately owned (1985: 84). A market economy of competitive individualism and profit would give way to principles of interdependence and mutuality, embracing 'barter, potlatch and communality' at the local level (1985: 85). Material self-sufficiency would be matched by political autonomy and decentralization: 'the spreading of power to small and widely dispersed units' (1985: 91) with 'nothing done at a level higher than necessary' (1985: 94), with the village level particularly prioritized.

The social vision of bioregionalism is not altogether a comfortable one. There is a sometimes rather nostalgic and retrogressive fondness in bioregionalism for the ways of life of pre-modern cultures and the supposed original natives of particular bioregions. The notions of reinhabitation and ecosystem restoration that animate the bioregionalist ethic of living-in-place suggest that landscapes can be returned to some pristine and original state prior to human interference, a perspective that has drawn much criticism in recent years.[9] Sale looks back in the hope that the 'lore' of native cultures can be recaptured and reinstituted (1985: 45) and at the same time draws lessons from nature in making prescriptions for social arrangements.[10] All these elements tend to infuse bioregionalism with a reactionary spirit that risks putting wild nature ahead of human liberation and social justice. It has little to say about who might benefit from the old ways. But at the same time, bioregionalism has developed to accommodate arguments for urban reinhabitation; even Sale's 1985 iteration argues for breaking down the city/country binary. The pragmatic outlook of bioregionalism insists that the transition to an ecocentric worldview and lifestyle can start here and now. It links small moments of eco-consciousness – enjoying wildflowers in your backyard, a moment spent looking out from the top of a local hill – to more ambitious communal projects – getting together with neighbours to reintroduce salmon to a local river – and thence to wider social transformation. Bioregionalism is rarely simply a celebration of returning to the past *tout court*; by discursively focusing on specific places and practices, it leaves room for the renegotiation and reinvention of past and present which have often been developed poetically and creatively, for example in the work of poet and deep ecologist Gary Snyder (1990, 1995) and in studies of the pasts and futures of particular places.

We see in bioregionalism, then, support for O'Riordan's early argument that the 'classic ecocentric' utopia is 'the self-reliant community modelled on anarchist lines' (O'Riordan 1976: 307). The anarchist strand of radical ecology is even more evident in Bookchin's vision of an 'ecological community and a participatory democracy' (Bookchin 1988: 192). Bookchin was a political theorist and anarchist activist. His writings on the relationship between social and natural liberation go back to the early 1960s.[11] Like the deep ecologists, Bookchin was opposed to the instrumental use of nature and to narrowly human-centred philosophies. But as a critical social ecologist, he was sceptical about what he saw as 'mystical' and 'misanthropist' strands in some deep ecological philosophies (Bookchin 1988: 12). He argued that deep ecology too often adopted an uncritical biocentrism and failed to identify the ways in which capitalist structures of power and exploitation have historically set humans against nature and led to both alienation and environmental collapse.[12] Instead, he suggests that we understand nature as a complex and cumulative system of evolution that tends spontaneously 'toward ever more varied, differentiated and complex forms and relationships' (1988: 36). Humanity represents a kind of second nature within the first, the outcome of a particular line of evolution that has led to self-awareness and active subjectivity. Nature matters in its own right – it exhibits 'tendency...direction...purpose' (1988: 37). But only humans have the agency and moral capacity to understand and remake the world. On this basis, Bookchin was keen to endorse a revival of the best elements of Enlightenment thought that envisioned universal human liberation.

Bookchin examined the relationship between social systems of hierarchy and the human domination and exploitation of nature, locating the origins of domination in early forms of patriarchy. The exploitation of women by men, he argued, generated an instrumental orientation to relationships, which in turn gave rise to the instrumental use and despoliation of nature (1988: 56; see Merchant 1982 for a related discussion). For Bookchin, the apogee of instrumental reason and the domination of both humans and nature is reached when patriarchy solidifies into the nation state (1988: 66) and when mediated, representational forms of democracy remove decision-making from face-to-face communities (1988: 71). Only anarchist models of libertarian social organization, without a central state, can guarantee human freedom and well-being, and only an end to private property ownership can end human exploitation. Bookchin's social ecology attends to questions of social power in ways that are often neglected by deep ecology and argues that it is 'social reconstruction', rather than the veneration of nature, that can bring about a greener society: 'the harmonisation of nature cannot be achieved without the harmonisation of human with human' (1988: 171).

Bookchin is often critical of deep ecology, and likewise some analysts of radical green politics have positioned his social ecology outside the spectrum of a fully ecocentric politics (Eckersley 1992). But, like the deep ecologists, he was implacably opposed to reformist environmentalism and, as in Naess's articulation of deep ecology, insistent that the environmental crisis is an inevitable outcome of industrial capitalism

(Bookchin 1988: 160). Bookchin's vision of the ecological society as a 'confederal Commune of communes...shaped to conform with the ecosystem and bioregion in which it is located' (1988: 193) shares many features with the utopian proposals of bioregionalism. Bookchin sees decentralized and self-sufficient communities as the building blocks of sustainability. Reintegrating social and natural systems at the local level ensures that economies remain within resource limits and fosters an ecologically attuned and unalienated consciousness (1988: 192). Bookchin prefers the small city as the ideal size and type of community – human-scaled and rich in opportunities for political participation and self-development, the small city *polis* enables a 'lived, vital and deeply felt consociation' (1988: 176). Comprising small mutually supporting communes, municipalities would share land ownership and engage in face-to-face democratic discussions. Citizens would all take a share in collective work, but priority would be given to energy and technology use that could 'free human beings from needless toil' and ensure 'unstructured leisure time for self-cultivation as individuals and citizens' (1988: 196). Bookchin, then, adds another iteration of the decentralized green society to the radical visions produced by deep ecological politics and philosophy.

The value of the ecocentric utopia

Bookchin is one of many radical green thinkers to openly endorse the value of utopia to ecological philosophy and politics. He is a student of libertarian utopian traditions and a historian of utopian 'ideals of freedom' (Bookchin 1988: 95) from More to Fourier. Bookchin argues that there is a particularly intimate relationship between anarchist philosophy and the utopian imagination. All radical movements for change depend on clearly articulated, explicit future visions to stimulate the imagination and educate desire (1988: 197). There is no predetermined logic of history unfolding in the direction of human emancipation; societies have been made and can and must be actively remade with a conscious image of the better life in mind to give 'direction, hope, and a new sense of place in nature and society' (Bookchin 1982: 325). Andrew Dobson has also argued that the utopian capacity to produce and defend explicit images of the good society has been a crucial part of radical green politics. Even the most cautious green reformers, Dobson suggests, need 'a radically alternative picture of post-industrial society' or 'phantom studies of the sustainable society'. Ecological politics, he suggests, is dependent upon deep ecological 'visionaries' (Dobson 1995: 199). De Geus agrees that green utopias infuse environmentalism with 'useful ideas, enlightening images, [and] challenging perspectives'. They are a unique source of 'inspiration' to ecological thought and politics (De Geus 1999: 56).

Deep ecology suggests more than that utopias can be a source of inspiration. Ecocentric philosophy is innately, indissolubly utopian in the expressive and desiring sense. It proposes a richer, better and happier way of life in line with ecocentric values. Naess, it is true, was rather sceptical about utopian visions in environmental politics. But his philosophical inquiry into the meaning of the good life for humans with nature is fully infused with the desire to explore and recommend a better way of living. Devall and Sessions (1985) are more typical, asserting that deep ecology is intrinsically visionary and indicating a number of proposals for a sustainable society. They argue that green utopianism functions to (re-)educate desire, enabling people to distance themselves from contemporary values and learn to want a different way of life (1985: 176). Eckersley similarly argues that a visionary utopianism is an essential part of deep ecology. It provides a 'heuristic of future possibilities' and 'new ways of seeing' that stimulate the desire for change (1992: 186). Deep ecology is predicated on the possibility of a cultural leap towards a different way of being rooted in an alternative vision of the world. Green utopias propose new epistemologies and new kinds of understanding which have a potentially transformative effect.

Others, however, have been more critical of green utopias. Pepper (2005), for example, argues that the visions produced by deep ecological philosophy have tended to be not only nostalgic and conservative in their content, but rigid and prescriptive in their form. Naess was uncomfortable with blueprint-type utopian visions of an ecocentric society, arguing that 'green is dynamic and comparative, not absolute and idealistic' (1989: 161). And Dobson's endorsement of green utopianism is also somewhat ambivalent. If deep ecology's utopias are a necessary inspiration in green politics, they are also strongly associated with a lack of pragmatism in the green movement. As we have seen, deep ecology seeks a radical change of consciousness – but some political theorists argue that it lacks a model of material change. It assumes a universal appeal and makes its subject humanity as a whole. As Dobson argues, ecologism has often failed to identify a social group with an immediate interest in fundamental green change, or adequately connected its visions with everyday experience (Dobson 1995: 23, 148).

The desiring and expressive utopianism of deep ecology takes green hope beyond mainstream environmentalism and the limits to growth discourse. It opens up a new discursive space around the concept of ecocentrism and prompts a radical, critical rethinking of human relationships with nature. It introduces creative alternatives to Western models of well-being and the good society, emphasizing ecocentric equality, metaphysics and meaning, culture and consciousness. Other philosophies and cultural and social movements have explored the need for human embeddedness in the natural, even in the wild, world. But deep ecology is unique in linking the prospects for a transformed subjectivity and perception with roots in romanticism and transcendentalism to the scientific insights of ecology, and renewing them for an age of systemic and global environmental crisis. Deep ecology refuses to allow the environmental crisis to be chopped into discrete sets of problems that can be treated as the objects of instrumental or technocratic reason. It insists that environmental crisis is inseparable from questions of who we are and how we live. At the core of deep ecology, then, is a fundamentally utopian challenge. In its social and political proposals, radical ecology adds to this critical and desiring utopianism a substantive account of the world that might be. Ecocentric proposals sketch out the possibility of the good life rooted in small, decentralized, self-sufficient communities in touch with nature.

But if the content of deep ecology's vision is persuasive and powerful, its utopianism is nonetheless limited. This is partly related to the forms in which ecocentric ideas are usually expressed. On one hand, there are the normative discussions and ethical tenets found in deep ecological philosophizing. Abstracting from the complexity of lived social experiences, they propose statements about how the world ought to be, which can feel deeply detached from life in a decidedly non-ecocentric culture. On the other hand, there are the polemical visions of a decentralized society found in deep ecology's political proposals. Even the best of these, for example Sale's *Dwellers* – beautifully written, engaging and accessible – are prescriptive and descriptive, distant from the texture of everyday life and the way people live. Bioregionalist and eco-communal visions can specify how big a community ought to be, but the language of political persuasion offers little in the way of how it might feel to be stuck in a small, static community. Deep ecology can explain the logic of a decentralized politics and offer some different proposals for structures of participation, but can't tell us much about how we might live. Caught in abstract, descriptive and polemical modes, the utopian function of ecological critique and estrangement is limited. In the next chapter, I explore how green utopian fictions of the 1980s and 1990s turned arguments for a decentralized green society into a reading experience that embodies the fullest function of utopianism.

4

Utopian Fiction: Imagining the Sustainable Society

Reading ecotopian fiction

> And so the meeting rolled on, filling Wednesday night as so many meetings had before. A building permit battle that became a protest against town ownership of the land, a zoning boundary dispute, an ordinance banning skateboards on bike trails...all the business of running a small town, churned out point by point in a public gathering. The work of running the world, repeated thousands of times all over the globe; you could say that this was where the real power lay. But it didn't feel like that, this particular night in El Modeña – not to Kevin. For him it was just work, and dull work at that. [...] At about the fifth of these votes, he felt a strong sinking sensation – he was going to have to spend every Wednesday night for the next two years, doing just this! Listening very closely to a lot of matters that didn't interest him in the slightest! How in the *hell* had he gotten himself into it? (Robinson 1995 [1990]: 91)

In chapter 3 I showed how deep ecological philosophy and green political ideology express utopian desires for a more ecocentric culture and propose outlines for a sustainable economy and society. I argued that deep ecology is expressively powerful and its political visions are remarkably consistent in detailing the main features of the green society. I also suggested that deep ecology's philosophical and political proposals for a green society lack specificity and a practical feel for everyday social experience. They have a limited capacity to explore the texture of life in other, greener, worlds. In this chapter I argue that green speculative fiction is exceptionally good at engaging its readers in exactly this way. Utopian fiction doesn't have a very good reputation. People often think of it as being more polemic than literature: too much description of structures and not enough action, event and character. But utopian fiction can be a highly sophisticated form, creating a compelling relationship between text and reader, between the imagined experience of a better society and a subjectivity located in the world as it really is. Ecotopian novels can make our taken-for-granted unsustainable worlds seem problematic and contingent. Deep ecological tenets are worked up into rich descriptions of everyday experience. Blueprints and outlines for sustainability are brought to life and set in motion. Through plot, character and event rather than description, rationale and persuasion, green utopian fictions can help us understand what it might feel like to live in a more sustainable society.

For example, utopian fiction takes the ethical-political commitment to decentralized participatory politics of deep green philosophy and turns it into a new councillor sitting in a courtyard for the weekly town meeting, the trees hung with streamers and paper lanterns. He is bored and slightly drunk on 'Al Schroeder's atrocious champagne' (Robinson 1995 [1990]: 91). The experience of Kevin at that meeting, in the long quote above, is taken from Kim Stanley Robinson's novel *Pacific Edge*, first published in 1990. *Pacific Edge* is one of a number of green utopian novels from the second half of the twentieth century that presented lively, affecting visions of a better and more fulfilling life in an ecologically sustainable society. Earlier examples include *Woman on the Edge of Time* by Marge Piercy (1979; first published in 1976), and *Always Coming Home* by Ursula K. Le Guin (1986). Shaped by feminist and ecological ideas, these novels combine a radical critique of late industrial capitalism with a liberatory politics of gender and nature.

In this chapter I look closely at these three novels. They span a twenty-year period beginning shortly after the emergence of the limits to growth discourse, proceeding alongside the consolidation of deep ecology's visions, and ending as sustainable development was becoming mainstream. These fictions belong to a period in which environmentalism's futures were maturing and becoming more culturally visible. Their imagined future societies share much with deep ecology. Piercy explores autarkic social structures, conservationism and anti-hierarchical dynamics that resonate strongly with Bookchin's social ecology (1982, 1988). Le Guin and Robinson set their futures on the West coast of the US and explore aspects of the wilderness philosophy of Devall and Sessions (1985), as well as bioregionalist ideas (Berg and Dasmann 1977). All imagine what it would be like to live in small, self-reliant communities with stable-state economies after a radical break with capitalism. Each shows possibilities for local decision-making and political participation. They invent ecocentric cultures and dramatize environmentalist debates. Piercy and Le Guin create plots which turn on violent threats to their peaceful, post-industrial worlds from aggressive technocentric forces. Robinson explores the tensions between the intuitive green ethics and deep love of nature of his protagonist and the more pragmatic and reformist sustainable society in which he lives.

These ecotopian fictions are much more than simple illustrations of philosophical and political ideas. They transform and animate them. The first thing I look at in this chapter is theories of form relating to science fiction and utopian narratives that offer an insight into how these texts function and the effects they can have on readers. I go on to outline the utopian societies envisioned and the stories told in *Woman on the Edge of Time*, *Always Coming Home* and *Pacific Edge*. I then read some selected textual devices of the three novels more closely in order to examine their distinctive contribution to green utopianism. I draw on Moylan's (1986) argument that the utopian text's capacity to provoke estrangement and questioning reached a peak in these critical utopias of the 1970s, a set of formally innovative and politically radical science fiction texts that transformed the very nature of the utopian narrative. I also draw on accounts of the reading experience of utopian fiction (Ruppert 1986; Jameson 2005) to think about the process of engaging with utopian narratives in relation to social experience, identification and empathy.

Over the past thirty years, theorists including Williams (1978), Suvin (1979, 2010), Moylan (1986, 2000), Ruppert (1986), Ferns (1999), Parrinder (2000) and Jameson (2005) have written about the formal qualities and reading experiences of utopian texts. Very few studies, however, have focused exclusively on environmental utopian fiction.[1] At the same time, very few studies of environmental utopianism have attended closely to the question of (fictional) form. They have tended to focus on the political and philosophical content of green utopian visions, rarely distinguishing between novels, memoirs, planning blueprints and polemics (De Geus 1999). Thus the specific contribution that green narrative utopias are able to make to green futures and green hope has been rather overlooked. In this section I provide a foundation for my reading of ecotopian fiction by outlining arguments from critical literary and cultural theory, suggesting that speculative fictional texts estrange us from our sense that prevailing socio-economic arrangements are necessary and unquestionable. In the face of the ideological limits of late capitalism and its capacity to absorb utopian desire and sell it back to us through the commodity fetish, this unsettling, estranging quality of speculative fiction is particularly valuable.

At their most dramatic, literary theorists have argued that the utopian fictional narrative is really an exercise in showing, in detail, the impossibility of imagining a world that is genuinely different from our own. Jameson (2005) argues that in modern or postmodern capitalist societies, the ideologies of consumerism, liberal individualism, private property and economic progress limit even our wildest imagination and the most speculative forms of fiction. Following Jameson's logic, we can't really conceptualize a society in which humans are not at the centre; in which objects are not valued by their exchange value; in which time is not reducible to labour hours. On this reading, speculative and utopian fictions can only gesture at and grope for alternative possibilities. This doesn't mean they aren't important. They allow us to feel out the shape and texture of what is wrong and what is lacking in our worlds (Bloch 1986). The process of imagining how

we might live otherwise illustrates the contingency of existing social forms. When we lend our imagination to utopian
fiction, we participate in a kind of anti-anti-utopianism
(Jameson 2005: xvi). We demonstrate, against the prevailing
wisdom of our culture, that existing social arrangements are
not inevitable and that change is desirable.

This idea that speculative and utopian fictions work to
dislocate us from existing social arrangements is crucial in
Marxist-inspired approaches to science fiction criticism from
the 1970s onwards. Suvin offers some startling insights into
how the science fiction narrative works (1979, 2010). He
focuses on how the language of the science fiction text works
to invoke an alternative world, rather than to represent the
real one. Reading a science fiction text involves encounters
with sentences that fail to make immediate sense. Signifiers malfunction or make strange connections; it is hard to
work out where one is and what is going on. Unlike realistic
fiction, science fiction introduces what Suvin calls a novum –
a wholly new technology, a surprising social development, a
new planet or creature. This novum is only just representable
through existing linguistic forms. It forces a break between
words and the familiar properties of the world around us.
Introducing its novum, the science fiction text makes us
work to cognitively produce a new (temporary) ontology in
which the words might make sense. As we become drawn
into making this alternative world hang together, we become
estranged from the taken-for-grantedness of our own world.
The utopian text becomes a site of cultural resistance. The
image of any particular utopian society is less important than
the act of utopian imagination (Moylan 1986: 26).

For Suvin, all science fiction can have a utopian function,
even if it depicts an apparently worse society. The utopian
effect of cognitive estrangement frees up the reader from
what is, to contemplate what might and what should be.
Historically, however, novels that were formally utopian and
aimed to depict a better society have not always exhibited
this technique of plunging the reader immediately into a
strange new world. Utopian fiction has often used rather tired
tropes to introduce its perfect societies. Ferns (1999) explores
the way that utopian texts have used the device of a native
guide showing a visitor around their perfect society to convey
its exemplary social and economic structures, its marvellous

lifestyle. This can render the utopian world in a static and lifeless way. Characters are little more than stereotypes and archetypes. Narrative tension is reduced to the visitor's conversion to the self-evident benefits of the alternative society. Even in fictional forms, then, the figure of a utopian society can appear as a thin blueprint, and the experience of encountering it can lack life and interest.

Raymond Williams (1978), drawing on the work of French critic Miguel Abensour, contrasted systematic forms of utopian fiction with heuristic utopias. Systematic utopias sacrifice rich depictions of messy human life and explorations of values and well-being to detailed diagrams of economic structures and institutions. The heuristic mode, on the other hand, foregrounds the creation of an open and constantly changing utopian society, visibly made and remade by active, creative subjects. These texts are concerned not only with social and political structures, but also with embodying in an imaginative vision the substance of a new set of values and cultural forms. The heuristic utopia imagines a better society based on new ethics or principles, but it also considers the changes that brought that society into being and explores the utopian society as a living, changing entity. By inserting the utopia into (a fictional) history, the heuristic text foregrounds reflexivity and change. It invites the reader to re-interpret their own present and cultivate the utopian desire for something different, to embrace a processual openness towards change.

For many utopian critics, one of the best examples of this exploratory, desiring form of utopian fiction was William Morris's *News from Nowhere*, first published in 1890. Morris's book takes the reader through a dreamlike exploration of a pastoral socialist society and includes a long account ('When it Changed') of the cultural and economic revolution that brought it about. Morris's utopia, Thompson suggests, 'liberates desire to an uninterrupted interrogation of our own values, and also to its own self-interrogation' (Thompson 1975: 791).[2] Williams (1978) dwells on Le Guin's science fiction, especially her genre-changing *The Dispossessed* (1975), an 'ambiguous utopia' whose narrative moves between two contrasting planets (rich, unequal, individualistic, violent Urras, and barren, anarchist, communal and borderline repressive Anarres). *The Dispossessed* refuses to identify either planet straightforwardly as a utopia. For Moylan (1986), *The Dispossessed* is one of a group of twentieth-century science fiction texts that introduced a truly dynamic and processual form of utopian fiction. These critical utopias not only questioned contemporary social arrangements, but they criticized the static, structural forms of older utopian fictions. Their narratives engaged reflexively with utopian literary traditions and rejected the formal blueprint in order to preserve utopia's open-ended desiring, visionary qualities. Their plots foreground a conflict between the utopian and the originating world, offering a thematic focus on human agency in social transformation through eventful and often gripping narratives. And in the critical utopia, the utopian society itself is depicted as open, changing and imperfect.

For Moylan, then, some texts are better than others at providing opportunities for the reader to untangle herself from ideology and taken-for-granted ideas and learn to want something different. Some novels do a better job of reflecting on the utopian form and building new kinds of narrative that can develop rather than constrain the expression of ideals of equality, emancipation and ecocentrism (see also Ferns 1999). The function of the fictional utopian text is not to provide a recipe for a viable green or post-capitalist future society. Sophisticated, reflexive utopian texts instead offer a heuristic for interpreting the problems of our own world and allow us to explore what kind of alternative we might want. Only one of the novels I discuss in this chapter is included in Moylan's selection of critical utopias: Piercy's *Woman on the Edge of Time*.[3] But Le Guin's later novel *Always Coming Home* and Robinson's utopia *Pacific Edge* constitute, I argue, examples of the critical utopia extending beyond its critical mass in the 1970s. Below I introduce the three novels as examples of critical utopianism, and link them to green and feminist themes in science fiction in the twentieth century.

Three ecotopias

Woman on the Edge of Time (1979) is widely recognized as an important feminist utopia. The novel is set primarily in

Mattapoisett, a village in future Massachusetts. Mattapoisett is one of many decentralized, small-scale, semi-rural settlements in the novel's green, egalitarian, multi-cultural, post-gender and anti-patriarchal future world. It is organized around a radically participatory democracy which includes representation for nonhuman beings. An economy based on organic agriculture provides for a society which enjoys a sophisticated culture and advanced technology. In Mattapoisett the nuclear family has been rejected in favour of technologies for extra-uterine conception and gestation. Co-parenting is undertaken by three friends and non-monogamous sex is for pleasure, not relationships. Communal life provides sociality and infrastructure for Mattapoisett's inhabitants; eating together in the communal fooder is particularly important. But Mattapoisettans also value individual spaces and time alone; everyone has a private living and sleeping room. Mattapoisettans accept the need for frugality and simplicity in some parts of their lives. But they also enjoy rich satisfactions and pleasures in their everyday lives; quality time with others is prioritized and parties and festivities are frequent.

The novel opens in the then contemporary world with a violent incident: Connie Ramos, a poor Latina woman, attacks her niece's vicious pimp and is committed to a psychiatric hospital. There she is visited by Luciente, a person from the future. As the connection between Connie and Luciente grows stronger, Connie is able to visit Luciente's utopian future world. The narrative moves between Mattapoisett in 2137 and New York circa 1979. The two worlds co-exist in what Moylan calls a 'pattern of mutual influence that spirals like a double helix beyond binary closure' (1986: 142). Connie's capacity for personal transformation and willingness to struggle against powerful oppressive forces in her own time are fed by her encounter with a future of ecological sustainability, freedom and justice. At the same time, the people of Mattapoisett need Connie to act for them in her present and enlist her 'help in the ongoing revolution to assure that a progressive line of history remains' (Moylan 1986: 142). At one point in the narrative, Luciente and her world 'blink out' (Piercy 1979: 229) and Connie is thrown briefly and bewilderingly into a glittering technotopia of gross sexual exploitation and environmental destruction. The novel never quite settles on whether the Mattapoisett future is real or a dream. Throughout, narrative tropes of science fiction and utopian fiction bleed into the sections set in Connie's New York world, just as the 'naturalistic detail' of the realistic register (Moylan 1986: 136) associated with Connie's present infuses future Mattapoisett.

Always Coming Home was published in 1986. Le Guin's multi-faceted, non-linear text takes the form of a fictional cultural anthropology of the Kesh, a 'people who might be going to have lived a long, long time from now in Northern California' (Le Guin 1986: xi). The Kesh way of life embodies and enacts an ecocentric cosmology; all human experience is infused with a sense of embeddedness in the natural world. This is organized by a carefully described cultural and cosmological system that celebrates human/nonhuman relationships and organizes social activities – through ritual, craft, and conversations with all living things – in ways that minimize impacts on nature. The novel describes the Valley way of life which is rooted in village structures. Agriculture is the central and communal economic activity and most villages are self-sufficient in staples (1986: 24). There is modest barter and trade with other regions. There is no production for profit and no monetary economy. Real wealth consists in the 'act of giving', not in accumulation (Le Guin 1986: 112). Valley society rejects linear and progressive rationality, especially the urge to accumulate and expand. It measures time in flows, gyres and cycles. In the Valley, 'owning is owing, having is hoarding' (1986: 313).

Always Coming Home is a formally innovative text that combines fictional anthropological documents with several powerful stories. A central narrative concerns Stone Telling, a young Kesh woman who leaves her Valley home to live with her father and his non-Kesh tribe, the Condor. Stone Telling's story stages a conflict between the Kesh way of life and our own, presented allegorically via the Condor, whose civilization legitimates conceptual binaries and the hierarchical domination and exploitation of other people and the nonhuman world. But Stone Telling's story is interrupted, expanded and even undermined by the text's presentation of other stories and fragments from Valley life. Through and around Stone Telling's story, *Always Coming Home* weaves a compendium of recipes, songs, folk stories, drawings and village maps apparently made by the Kesh themselves. There are also excerpts from what might be an ethnographer's field notes detailing Kesh cultural systems and beliefs, and reflections from a narrator, referred to as Pandora, who critically comments on the form of utopia and suggests to the reader some possible relationships between the ecocentric life of the Valley and our own times.

Robinson's *Pacific Edge* (1995), first published in 1990, is the third part of a science fiction trilogy, each part projecting a different alternative future set in Orange County, California. Often melancholy in tone (James calls it a 'sad' utopia; 1992: 123), *Pacific Edge* nonetheless offers a utopian counter to the two earlier novels, *The Wild Shore* (1994, first published 1984), which explores a bleak post-holocaust scenario, and *The Gold Coast* (1993, first published in 1988), a dystopian vision of a gleaming automotive, military-capitalist technotopia. *Pacific Edge* paints a vivid picture of everyday life in a sustainable society which combines high technology, social justice, local sustainability and an almost cartoonishly healthy outdoor lifestyle. El Modeñans live with groups of friends and family in communal apartments, sharing domestic and childcare responsibilities, and growing some of their own food. Kevin and his friends pursue professions and undertake modest amounts of paid work alongside several hours' town work every week. Each citizen is entitled to a share of the town's income. In Robinson's sustainable future there are legal limits on company size and the economy is a mixture of small-scale private enterprise and municipal businesses. Land and utilities are publicly owned and development is carefully controlled. El Modeña and its citizens are all comfortable but none are enormously wealthy.

The narrative of *Pacific Edge* concerns the growing up of Kevin Claiborne as he comes to terms with the death of his grandfather and the winning and then losing of the love of his life. These events play out alongside a political plot in which Kevin fights to save Rattlesnake Hill, the last piece of wilderness in the local area. The environmental pragmatists of the novel's New Federalist party want to develop the land to serve the community's need for amenities and jobs. Kevin and the Green Party want to preserve the hill as a symbolic and material embodiment of the green ethos they feel is increasingly lacking in the town's life. As the novel unfolds, Kevin's deep feeling for his native wild landscape and his intuitive ecocentric ethics are pitted against the modest, progressive and rational model of sustainability that has been achieved in El Modeña and beyond. Robinson's text explores the complexities of this relationship between what Jameson (2005) calls utopian programme and utopian desire, between the materialization of a particular utopian dream and a looser, more open-ended desire for the good (see also Harvey 2000). Robinson deploys an understated naturalistic style, juxtaposing explanations of the economic and legal transformations that have made Kevin's world with the small joys and disappointments of his everyday experience. People in *Pacific Edge* are often bored and tetchy, stuck in tedious social situations or falling out with friends. Or, like Kevin, they are desperately unhappy. Utopia is not a solution to personal woes. But on a day-to-day basis, the citizens of El Modeña keep making the decisions to keep hope and the good alive.

These brief sketches give some idea of the three novels. But their historical and genre contexts are also important, especially in terms of understanding their ecological ideas. All three novelists have made significant contributions to extending science fiction in relation to the exploration of social, political and anthropological themes. Across their extensive bodies of work, Le Guin and Robinson have both challenged the hard science/humanist binary that once framed science fiction criticism (Clute 2015). The three novels I discuss here are also part of the outpouring of feminist science fiction in the 1970s and 1980s in the US and Europe (Johns 2012; Merrick and Tuttle 2015). Piercy's text was one of the earliest of those texts. Many critics have argued that the speculative narratives and non-realist genre conventions of science fiction gave feminist writers a particularly valuable fictional space for exploring critical and oppositional ideas at this time. This moment of intersection between feminism, utopia and science fiction has been very well studied (Bammer 1991; Haraway 1991; Sargisson 1996; Johns 2012; *inter alia*), although there has been a tendency to reduce the environmental ideas of these novels to an element of their feminism.

By the 1970s, science fiction was renewing an already established tradition of writing on ecological themes. Throughout the twentieth century, science fiction and fantasy had imagined near and far future ecosystem collapse, invading alien ecologies, and the colonization and terraforming of other planets (Stableford 2015). Depictions of utopian relationships between nonhuman nature and human societies have featured strongly in fantasy writing, often pastoral or Edenic in tone, set in a pre-industrial world of organic harmony. Apocalyptic science fiction had imagined much simpler post-holocaust worlds in which the survivors learned to rely anew on a depleted earth. In the 1960s, eco-dystopias had emerged showing fictional futures characterized variously by food shortages, population explosions and authoritarian politics; by the crass commercialization of nature and decadent squandering of environment resources; and by mysterious events in which nature runs wild. The three novels discussed here reconfigure these themes in very distinctive ways by confronting the prospect of systemic, human-made environmental crisis, elaborating on themes derived not just from ecosystems science, but from ecopolitical philosophy, and expressing both the warning of limits and the insights of the emancipatory ecology discussed.

These novels also respond to questions of sufficiency, development, justice and nature addressed through the longer history of utopian fiction. More's *Utopia*, published in 1516 and in part a response to the violence and poverty of Tudor England, suggested a simple but comfortable existence carefully balanced between agricultural stability and economic development. As modernity progressed, the tension between utopias of abundance and utopias of sufficiency (De Geus 1999) became more marked, however. Utopias depicting economic expansion and technological development diverged from those imagining the limitation or reconfiguration of human wants in relation to natural systems and modest production (De Geus 1999: 21–2). This contrast is very visible in relation to two competing visions of the nineteenth century. Morris's *News from Nowhere* presented a medievally influenced Arcadia with small-scale craft work and communal life. Urban and industrial structures were gently overtaken by organic growth. Bellamy's *Looking Backward* represented the socialist future via metaphors of the machine and with the assumption that perfect economic efficiency would enable human happiness. Around the same time, Gilman's *Herland* described a society of women living entirely in harmony with a pastoral landscape; and in the 1960s Huxley's *Island* anticipated emerging environmental ideas by combining Eastern spirituality with a critique of industrial modernity. All these novels provide material to be worked and reworked in the green utopias of the 1970s to the 1990s.

Green utopias: critical and experiential

One of the main ways in which the green utopian novels I discuss here are distinctive is in their use of the critical narrative strategies identified by Moylan (1986) to deconstruct the ideologies of late capitalist modernity and progress in order to create a space for imagining a post-industrial green society. In order to do so, they often play with generic features of science fiction and utopian texts, unpacking and twisting them to create surprise and cognitive estrangement. Moylan (1986: 16; see also Jameson 2005 for later developments) argues that by the 1970s capitalism had almost entirely colonized the utopian form so that technocentric dreams of abundance dominated, and mainstream ideas of the future simply affirmed ideologies of economic expansion, inequality and the commodity fetish. For green utopian texts seeking to (re-)articulate utopianism with the ethics of ecology and sufficiency, this relationship between abundance and utopia had to be deconstructed. *Woman on the Edge of Time*, *Always Coming Home* and *Pacific Edge* all enact this contradiction within their highly self-reflexive narratives.

In *Woman on the Edge of Time* (1979), the reader finally arrives with Connie in Mattapoisett, after several visits from Luciente.[4] This scene works to great effect by layering and juxtaposing multiple possible futures and remembered pasts. Connie, expecting 'skyscrapers', 'spaceports' and 'glass domes' finds only 'old wood, old bricks and stone' made into small, ramshackle homes overrun with vegetation (Piercy 1979: 68). Connie arrives in Luciente's future with what Ross has called the 'semiotic ghosts' (1991: 101) of a progressive futurist discourse that dominated modern Western imaginaries in the mid to late twentieth century, not least through science fiction. Looking at Mattapoisett through this lens, Connie cannot even recognize it as the future; maybe, she thinks, 'we blew ourselves up and now we're back to the dark ages' (Piercy 1979: 68). More specifically, it reminds her of her family's immigrant past:

> Goats! Jesus y Maria, this place is like my Tío Manuel's back in Texas. A bunch of wetback refugees! Goats, chickens running around, a lot of huts scavenged out of real houses and white folks' garbage...all that striving and struggling to end up in the same old bind? Stuck back home on the farm...That's where my grandparents scratched out a dirt poor life! It depresses me. (1979: 70)

Connie eventually accepts Mattapoisett, symbolically giving her lost daughter Angelina to this 'Podunk' (1979: 70) future. Knitting family trajectories and social progress into a weave of possible futures, dystopian fears and utopian hopes, *Woman on the Edge of Time* works hard to disconnect Connie – and us – from the normative ideals of our time, referred to in the novel as the 'Age of Greed and Waste' (Piercy 1979: 151).

The narrative of *Woman on the Edge of Time* moves the action between different pasts, presents and futures. As it does so, its characters reflect on social history and personal memories. The text dramatizes the limits of the modern, linear notion of progress at the same time as it foregrounds the centrality of human agency in social change. This theme is taken up even more strongly by Le Guin in *Always Coming Home*. In her critical writing, Le Guin has discussed how the discourse of progress treats time according to a spatial imaginary, converting the future into a place that can be colonized by contemporary expansive values (Le Guin 1989: 87).[5] This one-way, blinkered notion of the future is a function of modern rationalities which fetishize planning to impose the will of the powerful on the world. Le Guin's strategy in *Always Coming Home*, then, is to remove her imagined people, the Kesh, from our history, insisting instead that they 'have always lived there' (1989: 99). All three novels include signifiers of late capitalist infrastructures and ideologies and the rationalities of modernity itself within their texts and even within their utopian worlds. Piercy explores, through Connie, the powerful dreams of capitalism. She presents Mattapoisett and other ecotopian villages in her future fighting off aggressive military forces at the edges of their world and continuing to repair environmental damage and look forward to a time 'when the oceans will be balanced and the rivers flow clean, when the wetlands and the forests flourish', as Luciente says (Piercy 1979: 328).

In *Always Coming Home*, the remains of our world persist into the Valley in the form of the material detritus of a long, slow apocalypse and as an ever-present epistemology and will to power that threaten the Kesh's dreamworld. The Kesh tell stories about the risk of stumbling into our world, the City of Man, which is their nightmare. Here the air is 'thick and yellow', the food is poisoned, the road is 'coated with grease and feathers' (Le Guin 1986: 155–6). In *Pacific Edge*, our world intrudes into the culture of the future in an ironic register. In one episode, Kevin and his friends visit a still semi-urban Los Angeles where they encounter a version of our own late capitalist culture played as lifeless postmodern kitsch: in the 'historical district' of Bishop people can eat at a coffee shop called Huk Finn's or visit an old-style auto shop (Robinson 1995: 193). Robinson allows us here to recognize our own world as anachronistic and hollow in comparison to the vibrant everyday life of El Modeña.

But none of the three novels presents its smaller, more modest future society as a return to a simpler and happier time. The narrative strategies that enable the texts to deconstruct the linear model of progress also work to unsettle the problematic trope of the pastoral (Garforth 2005). The risk in representing ecocentric sustainability is to offer a regressive or romantic fantasy of a rural idyll, a myth of pre-industrial organic unity legitimating social conservatism, injustice and hierarchy. Robinson sometimes presents El Modeña in terms of the enduring, timeless qualities of the landscape, the harmony between its nature and its people, a culture that favours simple physical pleasures over an elaborate cultural or artistic sphere. But this is continually disrupted and even undercut by the commentary provided by El Modeña's most recent arrival Oscar, a sophisticated urbanite. His letters to Claire offer wry reflections on Californian beach culture, approaching the 'Arcadian' landscape and lifestyle with both affection and bemusement (Robinson 1995: 75). In *Always Coming Home*, the Kesh live a self-consciously simple life, embedded physically and culturally in the surrounding land-scape, with cyclical rhythms and stable and enduring social relationships. But in Le Guin's fragmentary text, static certain-ties and organic holism are frequently disrupted; the Valley is contextualized via stories of encounters with alien cultures; and the Kesh live in the Valley alongside semi-autonomous, self-perpetuating modes of technological life that they use but are not dominated by. In *Woman on the Edge of Time*, Mattapoisett balances small, settled societies with a vision of cultural diversity and fierce social equality. And Mattapoiset-tans would never countenance *not* using their limited technol-ogy and energy supplies to run dishwashers: this is a society of voluntary simplicity, not gendered drudgery.

All three texts also reflect on the nature of utopia itself, a key characteristic of the critical form (Moylan 1986). The fragments of text that make up *Always Coming Home* are (just) held together by the intermittent voice of Pandora, who addresses the reader directly and reflects on the difficulties of presenting their world from inside ours. Pandora's tone ranges through sincerity, irony and anger but it is dominated by worry. She firmly resists the rigid, blueprint mode of uto-pianism that presents images of 'static perfection' (Le Guin 1986: 87). She 'does not want to look in the big end of the telescope and see, jewel-bright, distinct, tiny and entire, the Valley.' She wants to start instead with '[b]its, chunks, frag-ments. Pieces of the Valley...a piece of madrone wood, a piece of obsidian' (Le Guin 1986: 53). Pandora worries that her utopian fantasy is simply escapist or compensatory, a 'mere dream dreamed up in a bad time...a critique of civili-zation possible only to the civilized, an affirmation pretending to be a rejection, a glass of milk for the soul ulcered by acid rain' (Le Guin 1986: 316).[6]

In *Pacific Edge*, Tom Barnard also worries about the rela-tionship between utopian dreams and the worlds in which they are produced. In Robinson's text, Kevin's life of sunny sustainability is occasionally interrupted by the reflections of a would-be utopian writer some fifty years earlier. Tom's world is 'maddened', 'slipping from crisis to crisis', beset by civil war, mass migration, climate change, deforestation and increasing nationalism (Robinson 1995: 257). As Tom contemplates the alternatives, he comes across utopian novels by Wells and conducts a one-sided argument with science fiction writer Samuel Delaney. He complains that the literary utopian form is 'static, ahistorical'; literary utopias 'don't speak to us, trapped in this world, looking at them in the same way we look at the pretty inside of a paperweight' (Robinson 1995: 81). Utopia feels like a withdrawal from the pain of the present, an escape, a 'cheat', an 'engineered fresh start' (Robinson 1995: 81). And yet he finds that he needs utopian desire to 'make the future seem more plausible to me', to pit imagination against barbarity and ideology. Deciding that utopia is simply 'when our lives matter' (Robinson 1995: 155), Tom eventually connects his utopian desire to his own life – his memories of a happy, protected safe Californian childhood; the camaraderie he finds in an internment camp – and hence to history. As the novel unfolds we learn that the utopian writer is Kevin's grandfather, one of a group of lawyer-activists who instituted the legal basis of the new sustainable world.

All these green utopian novels, then, resist the blueprint and explore the desire for a better way of living and being (Levitas 2010 [1990]). Rejecting the role of what Pandora (Le Guin 1986: 136) calls the 'smartass utopian…' ('so much healthier and saner and sounder and fitter and kinder and tougher and righter than me and my family and friends'), they remake the utopian text as a series of questions about how we might contest current arrangements and live differently with nature. They hint at past and continuing catastrophe in the margins of their texts, at dystopian or disintegrating societies that might still be in the future. But these hints foreground the possibility and necessity of human choice in the process of building an alternative future. As Moylan argued (1986), critical utopian texts move between an imagined future society and a version of our own. They foreground the individual and collective agency of people who make the change. In this movement they insist that we compare and critique; that we learn to be estranged from our own society.

In these novels, then, the attempt to imagine sustainability is complicated and ultimately enriched by an interrogation of the genre constraints of utopian literature, the memories of futures-past crystallized in science fiction, and the broader cultural discourses within which the future is habitually constructed. This interrogation allows the reflexive green utopia to dislocate the future from technocentric modernity's dominant models of progress, as well as from the conservative lure of escape into an imagined pastoral past. The critical strategies of these novels clear a space for the elaboration of a different kind of future. They go on to fill that space – tentatively, provisionally – with a utopian picture of ecological sustainability and a better life for human subjects in a closer and more equal relationship with nature. Although the critical dimension of these novels insists that the future must remain open to desire and change, each also describes an alternative green society. They show us its physical characteristics and patterns of social organization; its economic structures, its ways of life; its cultures and modes of interactions. They outline a green politics, a green education, green rites of passage. The three novels do this in a way that is very different from the thin sketches of sustainability we find in mainstream policy and ecophilosophical texts. They present their societies as diverse, dynamic and changing; they foreground complicated characters, their everyday lives and specific experiences.

In *Pacific Edge*, for example, Robinson describes the experiences and feelings that go with active participation in local, decentralized decision-making. He gives El Modeñan politics a quirky style: loquacious, even long-winded; informal, a bit drunk on occasion. The resource issues that often preoccupy the council are specific to arid northern California. Similarly, Robinson brings to life the material infrastructure of his imagined future. Kevin is a 'bio-architect' who specializes in turning twentieth-century apartment blocks inside out so that the 'dead, inert boxes' (Robinson 1995: 190) become open, multifunctional spaces in which communities of friends and family live alongside sophisticated soft technologies for solar air conditioning and waste disposal, 'banana trees and cinnamon bushes' (Robinson 1995: 32). El Modeñan homes aspire to be 'nearly self-sufficient little farms' (Robinson

1995: 81), blurring the boundaries between nature, technology and habitation. But they also reflect a bioregionalist sensibility and a desire to make daily life as beautiful, useful and rich as possible. A 'poet of homes' (Robinson 1995: 76), Kevin makes spaces embedded in and responding to their landscape.

Pacific Edge describes the distinctive structures of sustainability in El Modeña in ways that are always animated by the daily experiences of its characters. At the heart of *Pacific Edge* is Kevin and his existential and emotional experiences in relation to the wild nature around El Modeña. The novel's opening lines sweep a panorama across the snow-topped San Gabriel mountains, over blue foothills, and down to olive, avocado and lemon groves below. In this 'garden run riot, the dawn sun flushing the landscape every shade of green' (Robinson 1995: 280), Kevin is walking down a hillside trail. At the end of the novel Kevin is restored to this scene, carving his initials into a rock on Rattlesnake Hill. As the novel opens and closes, then, Kevin appears as a figure in the landscape. But through the novel we share his sensuous and spiritual experience of El Modeña. Its 'braided smell' – 'orange blossoms, cut with eucalyptus, underlaid by sage' (Robinson 1995: 38) – stimulates moments of intense connection and exchange between human consciousness and nonhuman life, as when he cycles home after the council meeting described above:

> He knew the configuration of every dark tree he passed, every turn in the path, and for a long moment rushing along he felt spread out in it all, interpenetrated, the smell of the plants part of him, his body a piece of the hills, and all of it cool with a holy tingling. (Robinson 1995: 28)

In *Always Coming Home*, Le Guin uses lists and litanies to convey the quiddity and diversity of the northern Californian landscape, its 'sweetshrub and oceanspray and yellow azalea, the wild rose and the wild vine' in the rich land near the Valley creeks; the 'thick shrubs, digger pine, fir, redwood and madrone' in the sheltered canyons (Le Guin 1986: 50). Both *Always Coming Home* and *Pacific Edge* resonate with bioregionalist ideas about the value of wilderness and the need to (re)inhabit local landscapes. Wilderness is much more extensive in the world of the Kesh than in our own. The book is meticulous in documenting and describing the Kesh's many cultural systems for living in and with nature. Their cosmology makes careful distinctions between wild and domesticated or cultivated nature, between the Houses of Sky and the Houses of Earth. The concept of 'heyiya' is crucial. It expresses the pantheistic spirituality of the Valley (compared to the one-way, monotheistic worship of the Condor people), a sacredness of relationality. As Stone Telling explains:

> [i]f you gave Blue Rock nothing, what could it give you? If you never spoke to it, why should it speak to you? Easy enough to turn from it and say 'the sacredness has gone out of it.' But it was you that had changed, not the rock; you had broken the relation. (Le Guin 1986: 179)

Always Coming Home juxtaposes and layers up texts that suggest the anthropological details of Kesh life, presenting fragments of life as it is lived rather than describing structures. No-one discusses the politics of sufficiency, but we learn that in the Valley a house with seven cooking pots might be counted as rich. We learn about systems of agriculture, production and trade through texts called 'What they Wore in the Valley', or a long treatise on table manners, or a story about bartering with the Cotton People in a different valley. As well as documenting a way of life, *Always Coming Home* tells a life story. Though short and fragmented, Stone Telling's story provides a vein of autobiographical experience and personal reflections that bring the more ethnographic documents to life. The documents tell us that the Kesh give something – attention, care, notice – to all the elements of their landscape, and that they consider all entities to be 'people'. But Stone Telling shows us how she 'spoke to by name, or by saying "heya", the trees, fir and digger pine and buckeye and redwood and manzanita and madrone and oak, the birds, blue jay and bushtit' (Le Guin 1986: 20), and she tells us how she felt 'a long very thin string' connecting her soul to the Valley as she left it (Le Guin 1986: 189).

Piercy in *Woman on the Edge of Time* is less interested in wilderness as part of an ecocentric philosophy than Robinson

and Le Guin, and more explicitly concerned with the economics and politics of sustainability and the conditions for
social equality and personal liberation. The novel retains
some elements of the visitor-guide structure of utopian fiction
as well as troubling it, and the novel sticks more closely to
some of the descriptive tropes of utopian fiction than *Always
Coming Home* or *Pacific Edge*. Luciente, for example, gives
Connie a tour of 'Grandcil', the body of citizens (chosen by
lot) who deal with local resource distribution issues in Mattapoisett; here she meets the Earth and Animal advocates
who represent nonhuman voices in decision-making. Connie
accompanies Luciente as she goes about her work as a genetic
biologist and spends time in her humble one-roomed house
– which is nonetheless hooked into a powerful information
and communication network. They visit the brooder, where
soft aesthetics sit alongside the hard technologies of artificial
reproduction, and Connie sees the Mattapoisettan schools
where the children receive an education rooted in learning
their local ecology.

But we also learn about the texture and experience of
Mattapoisettan life through concrete experiences. Food is
a particularly vivid example. Describing what utopians eat
allows the text both to convey a sensuous feel for sustainable living and to thematize and interrogate the question
of what counts as sufficiency. In Mattapoisett they aim to
be self-sufficient in food production. Although this means
less choice and sometimes simply less, more is squeezed
out of it. Mattapoisettans aim to have 'enough food, good
food, nourishing food' (Piercy 1979: 174). Connie eats
a meal of

> cold cucumber soup flavored with mint. Slices of a dark rich
> meat not familiar to her in a sauce tasting of port, dollops of
> a root vegetable like yams but less sweet and more nutty –
> squash? Young chewy red wine. (Piercy 1979: 172)

It contrasts with the solitary, meagre food she takes in her
New York apartment, and the wider sense in her real life
that despite the commodities and wealth that surround her
'there wasn't enough! Oh, not enough things, sure – not
enough food to eat, clothes to wear, all of that. But there

wasn't enough [...] to do. To enjoy' (Piercy 1979: 280). The different choices that have been made in Luciente's world – not to undertake agricultural exploitation of land that local people need for crops, for example – have consequences, as Connie discovers when everyone sits around at breakfast feeling miserable and tetchy without coffee when their limited supply runs out. But on the whole we leave Mattapoisett, like Connie, feeling well nourished and better able to understand the kinds of hard choices, but also the new pleasures that a life of voluntary simplicity might have to offer.

Inhabiting utopia

Through critical narrative strategies and the invitation to inhabit a more sustainable society, ecotopian fictions make a distinctive contribution to green hope. In terms of their content – steady-state economy, local self-sufficiency, decentralization and embeddedness – they flesh out and bring to life the proposals of deep ecology. At a formal level, these fictions do something distinctive to our capacity to imagine new social-natural relationships. The ecotopian novel does not offer didactic proposals, sketch blueprints or make an appeal to logic, ethics or values. Its power lies in its narrative capacity, drawn from the distinctive devices of science fiction and the critical utopia, to unsettle and estrange the everyday. The novels enact critical deconstructions of the ideologies of exploitation and domination of the natural world that are more powerful than straightforward ecocriticism because of their ability to shake us out of our complicity in those ideologies. At the same time the novels have a descriptive capacity to present an alternative society through recognizable subjects, their experiences and everyday lives. Its fictional devices invite identification with and empathy for the particularities and contingencies of daily life in an imagined green world. It is their capacity to offer experiential and affective rather than simply cognitive approaches to sustainability that can build a bridge between our reality and the green utopian worlds of Piercy's Mattapoisett, Robinson's El Modeña and Le Guin's Valley.

Fictional green utopias in dialogue with radically ecocentric ideas offer powerfully unsettling and creatively inspiring engagements with an alternative future. Prescriptions for an environmentally sustainable and emancipated society are worked up into thick descriptions of daily life and subjective experience. These narratives help us to think about how it might feel to live in a different and more ecologically responsible kind of world. They enrich and diversify the principles of ecocentrism, positioning sustainable societies as worlds of possibility, not constraint and limits. De Geus (1999) argues that the green debate needs to be infused with a diversity of ideas about possible and desirable ecological lifestyles and institutions. He says that ecotopian heterogeneity is particularly crucial in relation to the deep green investment in the idea of ecological limits to growth, which so often is reduced to 'one-dimensional, bleak and austere' visions (1999: 269). Ecotopian novels provide a range of examples. They also animate the themes of choice, culture and empathy that have been so important in deep green philosophy. Rather than making sustainability a demand to which we must submit, they work to make it tangible and desirable.

Science fiction has continued to play speculatively with and in environmental futures to great effect (Otto 2012; Canavan and Robinson 2014). But after *Pacific Edge*, there have been few full-blown green utopian novels. This is not to say that there is no green utopianism in fiction and elsewhere – as we will see in chapter 5. Defined broadly as the desire for a better way of living with nature, we can find traces of green utopianism throughout literature and popular culture. Dystopias and post-apocalyptic narratives have arguably been particularly important in keeping green hope alive through the negative image of the prospects of a much, much worse society (Moylan 2000; Baccolini and Moylan 2003; Sargisson 2012). But since the high-water mark of ecotopian fiction in the 1970s and 1980s, the discursive framework of popular environmentalism has changed significantly. As I suggested in chapter 2, the sphere of environmental policy has shifted so that the language of sustainable development and approaches characterized as ecological modernization have dominated. As environmental ideas have become more mainstream, the radical calls for changes in culture and consciousness in ecophilosophy and deep ecology's proposals for steady-state sustainable societies have become less audible. The ideas of nature that animate the utopias of Piercy, Robinson and Le Guin have been criticized in audible theory, and the environmental crisis against which their ecotopian visions flourished seems to have become endemic in the early twenty-first century. In the next two chapters, I explore the prospects for green utopianism after the ecocentric utopian future and arguably after nature itself.

5
No Future: Green Utopias between Apocalypse and Adaptation

Rewriting crisis

Over the past twenty years or so, dominant Western constructions of the environmental crisis have shifted and the spaces of green hope are changing. In chapter 2 I argued that the idea of imminent but avoidable crisis was central to the articulation of the environmental problematic in the 1970s. In this period crisis narratives opened up new possibilities for imagining radical alternatives, stimulating a mood of green utopianism in ecological philosophy and the production of formal green utopias in political blueprints and speculative fiction. Here I argue that in contemporary environmental discourses the future no longer functions so well as a space for the projection of utopian desires or the description of green visions. The figure of environmental crisis is now less likely to appear as a spectre that could catalyse social change, and instead has come to suggest either total catastrophe or something that we are already living through. Environmental crisis is coming to seem either inevitable or ordinary, leaving the prospects for green hope at best changed and at worse hopelessly damaged.

For some commentators environmental crisis has become ordinary, a 'way of life'. It no longer, as Buell argues, looms ahead but is happening now in our homes and everyday experience (2003; see also 2010). In the early phase of post-war environmentalism, system-level problems were framed as future threats whose harbingers intruded into the present. Carson's *Silent Spring* described an American landscape denatured by DDT as a 'fable for *tomorrow*' (1999 [1962]; emphasis added). *The Limits to Growth* projected overshoot and collapse from 1972 over a 100-year run (Meadows et al. 1972). Radically ecocentric blueprints in the 1970s looked forward to the year 2000 (The Ecologist 1973). In the early 1990s Kim Stanley Robinson's post-apocalyptic and utopian green science fictions dreamed of a catastrophe in 2027 (Robinson 1993) and a better future in 2065 (Robinson 1995). That environmental predicament has now been absorbed into the present. Problems that would have seemed extreme projections fifty years ago are reported as unfolding right now. In just one month – August 2015, for example – you might see announcements of dramatic biodiversity loss (WWF 2015); reports on unprecedented damage to the world's forests (Sugden et al. 2015); and claims that changing patterns of mass migration linked to climate factors are becoming the 'new normal' (O'Hagan 2015).[1]

It is not only the increasing range, scale and intensity of reported environmental problems that positions crisis as normal. It is also the ways in which Western societies and cultures have begun to 'internalize' ecological knowledge, consciousness and understanding since the late twentieth century (Jamison 2001: 17; see also Barry 1999; Dobson 2009). Environmental issues are no longer framed as emergencies or radical challenges to the status quo, but rather as an ordinary part of late modern society and politics. Since the Brundtland Report (WCED 1987), the conceptual framework of sustainable development has asked international, national and local governing bodies to bring environmental issues into economic policy-making. Solutions to environmental problems focus on the everyday practices and mundane consumer choices of individuals and households, asking us to change how we travel to work or dispose of our waste. Businesses large and small have adopted green technologies and made innovative green products.

But if in some respects environmental crisis has been normalized and internalized, we are at the same time seeing a re-inscription of crisis in the form of climate change. In some ways climate change reiterates and amplifies the figure of crisis that has structured ecological debate since the 1960s. Global scientific bodies and policy-makers have measured carbon emissions and modelled temperature rises, predicting future systemic effects and warning that potentially dangerous changes will result from economic and industrial business as usual. In other ways, though, climate change is rewriting the crisis narrative. Its distinctive temporal logics frame the future in new ways. Carbon and methane particulates that will trap heat energy in the atmosphere for hundreds of years to come have already been emitted. Even if the rate of emissions were to dramatically drop tomorrow, warming processes caused by past emissions would drive temperature rises for hundreds of years.[2] In this sense the future has been written and we are locked into dynamics already underway.

In another sense, crisis threatens to become banal, a 'new norm' (Buell 2010: 28). Stories and images of horrifying climate events rehearsing the end of civilization have become common, even mundane. Apocalyptic images of melting ice caps, dried-up lakes and violent hurricanes accumulate across news media; end-of-the-world narratives proliferate in young adult fiction, blockbuster movies and tabloid newspapers. Our culture, as Palmer argues, has acquired the 'habit of apocalypse', forming a narrative tradition that can easily 'degrade...into routine' (2014: 159). Policy discourses have also arguably made climate change normal by focusing on the prospects for managing climate effects through moderate changes to human behaviours and socio-economic systems. The two most important terms framing climate governance are 'mitigation' and 'adaptation'. Mitigation policies focus on how to curb the worst excesses of the human activities that cause carbon emissions. Adaptation policies aim to support adjustments and build resilience so that communities can live with warming effects. Both suggest that the climate problematic can be addressed without significant changes to late capitalism and especially neoliberal commitments to economic growth. Policy discourses have met the challenge of climate change in a pragmatic mood that militates against the imagination of alternatives that are fundamentally different from the present.

This chapter works through some of these shifts in environmental discourse, exploring how recent framings have reconstructed crisis and eroded the capacity of the future to work as a space for imagining alternatives or cultivating green utopian desires. It is structured around two loosely defined and apparently opposed dynamics: apocalypse and adaptation. The first, apocalypse, captures the ways in which some scientific and many popular climate change narratives suggest that there may be no future at all, or that catastrophic climate changes are inevitable. Global warming dynamics are already in train and we have passed the point of stopping temperature rises; previous attempts to govern emissions have been unsuccessful or too weak from the outset. In such contexts, the future seems closed to change, agency and desire. It is always already too late to do anything; fatalism and 'eco-political pessimism' are widespread (Hulme 2009: 309). If 'the climate has always already been changed' (Canavan 2014: 5), the future seems to have collapsed into the present. But figuring apocalyptic or dystopian futures is not the enemy of hope. Apocalypse narratives are also about radical change; the necessity for change; about change that might happen despite our (worst and complicit anti-environmentalist) selves (Canavan 2014: 13). In this sense they may also be part of the (muted, limited) green utopianism currently possible.

The second strand of this chapter extends the idea of adaptation from its narrow policy meanings to refer to a wider set of discourses suggesting that the future will not, should not, or cannot be fundamentally different from today. This discourse is powerfully present in policy responses to climate change, but it also plays out in the banalization of crisis in media representations of climate change. Here, there is no future in the sense that there is no capacity to think in terms of a fundamental break with the present. We saw in chapter 2 that by the mid-1980s there had been a major shift in the dominant environmental discourse which began to conceive of the future in terms of continuities with present economic structures and ways of life instead of with reference to crisis, limits and radical change. These currents have continued as sustainable development remains the dominant framework for environmental policy-making and, as the language of adaptation and mitigation dominates, similarly frames climate change. The future seems to be colonized by the present. But the capacity for utopian desire does not entirely depend upon conceiving of the future in terms of radical change. A modest, grounded and pragmatic utopianism can thread its way through small actions, keeping open the possibility of surprising change. In the hands of a utopian science fiction writer, adaptation can even be figured as radically transformative.

In this chapter, then, I look at what kinds of green utopianism might be possible in the context of a strange new tension between the banalization of environmental crisis and the apparent inevitability of the end of the world. Amsler has called this the 'urgent but oddly bearable' shadow cast by environmental crisis in the early twenty-first century (2010: 129). The new phase of environmental concern reflects a growing consensus on climate change and the embedding of environmental problems in political decision-making, everyday practice and mainstream culture. But the internalization of ecological consciousness and concern also produces ambiguities. Environmentalism, as Jamison puts it, is 'decomposed', even 'reinvented' (2001: 17). It becomes more visible, mainstream and diffuse – but also less radical, less coherent and more detached from concrete hopes for a better future with nature (Dobson 2009; Giddens 2011).

Green utopianism persists in these conditions, but in new forms and with new functions. The formal ecotopian visions of sustainable societies discussed in previous chapters are thin on the ground, and full-blown political proposals for alternative futures are notable by their absence. Green hope does not disappear, however. It shifts into the present, or depends upon a paradoxical acceptance of the inevitability of major catastrophe. It becomes perhaps more modest and more compromised, but may also speak more of process and possibility. It becomes more thoroughly entwined with tropes of apocalypse and catastrophe, and its formal expressions depend more on dystopia and realism. But it persists.

I begin by tracing the policy framework on climate change that emerged in the United Nations Framework Convention on Climate Change (UNFCCC) in 1992, focusing on the language of adaptation and mitigation. Over the next fifteen years there was a solidification of the scientific consensus that climate change is real, anthropogenic and consequential. I look at how the future scenarios of the Intergovernmental Panel on Climate Change (IPCC 2000; see also 2001, 2007) have shaped ideas about the governability of climate. Recently, more chaotic climate scenarios have loomed larger in climate science and policy – as they have done for rather longer in mainstream debate, in fiction and in media. In the second section of the chapter I focus on the issue of abrupt climate change scenarios and on populist figures of climate chaos and apocalypse, asking whether catastrophic visions must mean indifference, political conservatism and collective fatalism.

In the final part of the chapter I consider where we might find green literary utopianism when speculating about the future is both more urgent and more unpromising than ever before. I look at the prospects for imagining utopia in relation to both adaptation and apocalypse in contemporary science fiction. It is widely recognized that utopian desire can be expressed through dystopian and even post-apocalyptic forms (Penley 1986; Booker 1994; Moylan 2000, 2003; Sargent 1994). Dystopian and post-apocalyptic settings can share the function of estrangement with formal utopian fictions, using the model of a worse society or the aftermath of a catastrophic collapse to shake up the commonsense of familiar social realities. Working within 'a dystopian structure of feeling' that may be necessary to their time (Moylan 2003: 149), speculative texts can warn of what will happen if things go on as they are; reveal alternative historical possibilities; and cultivate utopian hope for a better way of being. As Moylan notes, the three critically utopian authors I discussed in chapter 4 all 'revisited utopian politics and poetics in a dystopian mode' in later texts (Moylan 2003: 149). In this chapter I return to the work of Kim Stanley Robinson. I extend Trexler's (2015) analysis of his Science in the Capital trilogy as a speculative exploration of bureaucratic agency to read it as a green utopia of adaptation. I also turn to a more recent voice in environmental science fiction, Paolo Bacigalupi. I follow Otto's (2014) reading of his short stories to examine how the formally dystopian novel *The Water Knife* enacts critical green hope in the midst of an apocalypse that may be immanent rather than imminent.

Coming to terms with climate change

> Climate change is everywhere...The idea that humans are
> altering the physical climate of the planet through their col-
> lective actions...[is] as ubiquitous and as powerful in today's
> social discourses as are the ideas of democracy, terrorism or
> nationalism...It is an idea circulating anxiously in the worlds
> of domestic politics and of international diplomacy. It is an
> idea circulating with mobilising force in the worlds of busi-
> ness, of law and of international trade. It is an idea circulat-
> ing with potency in the worlds of knowledge and invention,
> of development and...circulating creatively in the worlds of
> art, of cinema, of literature, of music and of sport. (Hulme
> 2009: 322–3)

In this section I follow Hulme's argument above that since
the mid-2000s the world has (belatedly) been coming to
terms with climate change. There are still debates to be had
about the reliability of forecasts, the social co-construction of
climate models, and the limited range of narratives framing
our understanding of climate futures (Hulme 2009; Swyngedouw 2010; Doyle 2011; Urry 2011). Acknowledgement
of a changing climate is not straightforward: it continues
to be met by denial and rejection (Stengers 2015; Dobson
2016) and is also accompanied by apprehension, pragmatism,
terror, fatalism, indifference. Nonetheless, the science is as
certain as it can be. We are starting to understand what it
is like to live with a changing climate, and our ideas of the
future are changing too.

Hulme notes four moments that were part of a turning
point on climate change in the mid-2000s – away from language of equivocation, denial and delay and towards a focus
on certainty, acceptance and solutions (2009: 330–2). The
publication of the Fourth Assessment Report of the Intergovernmental Panel on Climate Change in 2007 was one
milestone. It announced on the basis of the best scientific evidence that warming of the climate system was 'unequivocal',
and that most of the observed increases in global temperatures since the mid-twentieth century were 'very likely' due
to increases in greenhouse gas emissions caused by human
activities (IPCC 2008: 30, 39). The Bali Climate Change Conference, also 2007, seemed to achieve success in negotiating

a road map towards a stronger regime for controlling emissions and supporting adaptation measures in developing nations than the initial commitments of the Kyoto Protocol (adopted in 1997; entered into force in 2005).[3] In 2006, the Stern Review outlined a comprehensive economic case for tackling climate change as a matter of urgency, and Gore's *An Inconvenient Truth* put climate change squarely into the media spotlight. Hulme argues that these moments created a new reality relating to climate change. They also reflected an increasingly embedded realism around the problem. If there was in the mid-2000s a (partial) consensus on the gravity of climate change and a sense that it could be tackled through urgent multilateral action, it was shaped in governance terms that reflected existing cultural and political assumptions and a vision of the future as continuous with the present.

The language of mitigation and adaptation has been central to the 'commonsense' (Taylor 2014: 64; see also Orlove 2009: 131) of international policy-making on climate change and crucial to making climate change a governable problem. Its roots are in the United Nations Framework Convention on Climate Change (UNFCCC). The UNFCCC sought to establish changes to the climate as a 'common concern of humankind' (UN 1992: 2) while simultaneously acknowledging the historical role of developed countries in producing greenhouse gas (GHG) emissions and anticipating the need of developing countries to increase them (UN 1992: 6). It called for 'cooperation' among countries, but also recognized 'differentiated responsibilities and...capabilities' linked to unequal social and economic conditions (UN 1992: 2). Its principal objective was the 'stabilization of greenhouse gas concentrations in the atmosphere at a level that would prevent dangerous anthropogenic interference with the climate system' (UN 1992: 2). Countries should 'take precautionary measures to anticipate, prevent or minimize the causes of climate change and *mitigate* its adverse effects' (1992: 9; emphasis added) and 'cooperate in preparing for *adaptation* to the impacts of climate change' (UN 1992: 11; emphasis added).

In 1992 the focus was primarily on mitigation and controlling emissions. Responsibilities for mitigation were primarily seen as belonging to developed nations (Annex 1 countries) (Hulme 2009; McKibben 2009; Dobson 2016). By 2007 the inevitability of atmospheric impacts was becoming clear and the focus shifted to encompass adaptation and the emerging consequences of warming for vulnerable non-Western (Annex 2) nations. In some ways then, the policy goals of adaptation and mitigation are in conflict, and in the period up to 2007 there were difficult disagreements about adopting an explicit focus on adaptation. On one hand, accepting the need for adaptation policies suggested a failure of mitigation attempts, a failure of Western developed nations to do their part – and also risked allowing those failures to dominate the conceptual terrain of climate policy, leaving it defensive and hopeless. Continuing to focus on mitigation, however, risked neglecting the pressing needs of vulnerable nations and communities. These were very real tensions that have had material impacts on responses to global climate change over the past few decades. But they also tend to obscure an equally important commonality relating to goals of continuity and modification in both adaptation and mitigation policy discourse. The first definition of adaptation as a policy goal described it as 'adjustment in natural or human systems in response to actual or expected climatic stimuli or their effects, which moderates harm or exploits beneficial opportunities' (IPCC 2001: Glossary). Mitigation, referring to policies and measures to limit GHG emissions, invokes ideas of qualification and extenuation; of management and control. Both respond to climate change as a process that cannot be fundamentally altered but that can be predicted, managed and adjusted to, and they construct policy solutions in a frame of incremental reform.

For some critics, the separation of mitigation from adaptation in policy discourse has been important in making climate change governable (Taylor 2014). If mitigation comes to carry the weight of socio-economic and human causes, adaptation can be treated as something that focuses solely on natural or environmental impacts. The anthropogenic causes of climate change are partly effaced and hazards are treated as external and natural (Hulme 2008: 1). This is intensified by the 'cultural baggage' (Orlove 2009: 136) that the term adaptation carries over from its association with evolutionary biology (Taylor 2014) and ideas of species survival and small fixes. Adaptation works with a thin notion of the social (Hulme 2008; Orlove 2009; Taylor 2014), leaving out complexities of culture and issues of power and justice. The very idea 'impos[es] considerable restrictions on the ways in which we can conceive of social transformation in an era of rapid climatic change' (Taylor 2014: 65). It imagines that human resourcefulness and resilience will enable adjustment to intensifying climate threats rather than demanding radical socio-economic change. It takes the politics out of climate responses. The language of adaptation suggests that a singular and inevitable warming future is unfolding in the form of a slow natural disaster that we must pragmatically accommodate.

Mitigation policies, on the other hand, have used multiple future scenarios to predict likely GHG emissions pathways and devise ways of stabilizing them below the threshold of 'dangerous atmospheric impacts' (UN 1992: 2). What Boykoff et al. (2010) call the myth of climate stabilization might be read as a technocratic response to the logics of climate change. If annual GHG emissions contribute to cumulative concentrations for years to come, then concentrations must peak before they can fall. Mitigation policies have therefore tended to try and set emissions restrictions in the present by projecting forward to imagine a plausible but notionally safe level of GHG rises in the future, and then 'work back to what emissions scenarios will get the world to that concentration' (Boykoff et al. 2010: 58). Mitigation policies colonize the future with multiple scenarios that suggest we can make logical, efficient choices between stabilization points and efface the extent to which these choices depend on political challenges and debates in the present.

The baseline emissions scenarios presented in the IPCC's (2000) *Special Report on Emissions Scenarios* (the 'SRES' models) have been particularly important in effecting this colonization of the future.[4] SRES produced four broad storylines mapping 'divergent' futures characterized by nominally different demographic, socio-economic, technological and environmental developments (IPCC 2000: 3). For each, they estimate effects in terms of GHG emissions, GHG atmospheric concentrations and global temperature rises.[5] Based on the SRES scenarios, the third and fourth IPCC reports projected global average surface warming and sea level rises to the end of the twenty-first century in the range of 0.6–4.0°C. Scenarios predicting business as usual with high economic growth and rapid technological development, especially those with continued dependence on fossil fuels, show the highest GHG concentrations and quickest temperature rises. Scenarios predicting cleaner growth and sustainable technologies appear to produce slightly lower GHG concentrations and later temperature peaks.

These scenarios were, as Hulme observes, crucial to establishing the 'physical reality of climate change' (2009: 325). But moving constantly between several different scenarios may make any particular warming future seem *less* real. Scenario projections allow policy-makers to translate complex, qualitative uncertainties about the future into linear, systematic paths. The future becomes an object for technocratic management (Boykoff et al. 2010: 62). We may assess some of the SRES storylines as being more realistic, others more hopeful. But the point is to offer multiple scenarios and development paths. They offer an illusion of rational choice between scenarios, a choice which is predicated upon erasing the social, moral, political and personal decisions and implications of each option. Discourses of mitigation, with the key metaphor of stabilization and the centrality of climate models, thus reinforce a 'delusion' of control and governance (Hulme 2008: 1). They promise to help us 'manage...for stability' (Jennings 2011: 240). Projecting a range of scenarios implies that choosing between them is a matter of rational choice, not a political challenge or an existential dilemma. Adaptation imagines climate change as an incremental process whose 'worst consequences' can be avoided by 'thoughtful preparation' on the part of wise policy-makers (Orlove 2009: 136). There is no space in either mode of looking ahead to the future for imagining a fundamental break with current institutions or ways of life.

Apocalypse now and always

Policy responses to climate change have been built on mapping future scenarios and seeking to establish measures for the stabilization of climate below the level of dangerous atmospheric impacts. As Boykoff et al. observe, climate science and policy up until the late 2000s worked together to construct a 'threshold between tolerability and unfettered disaster', conventionally set at a 2°C temperature rises (2010: 58; see also Swyngedouw 2010). Climate policy has focused on scenarios beneath the threshold where the future can be thought of as calculable and amenable to technocratic management. The discursive 'flipside' of governable climate change, however, is an 'insecure, unsafe, unstable' future (Boykoff et al. 2010: 61): climate chaos and catastrophe. Beyond stabilization there is no imaginable future, in the sense of the continuation of organized social life. I want to suggest here that the idea of catastrophe is an inevitable part of the ways in which contemporary Western cultures are imagining climate change. It is an unspoken but necessary part of the policy package: setting out the thresholds for manageable emissions also invokes the prospect of what lies beyond them. I want to suggest also that catastrophe might be an important part of the climate change imaginary. If Boykoff et al. are right that the ideal of technical management of climate change obscures its status as an ethical, political and even existential challenge (2010: 68), perhaps the idea of apocalypse lets them back in.

Since the mid-2000s, gradualist scenarios in climate science and policy have been complemented and perhaps even overshadowed by abrupt models (Gardiner 2010: 89). The SRES future scenarios (IPCC 2000) emphasized a relatively stable relationship between atmospheric GHG concentrations and steady rises in global surface temperatures. But we hear much more now about the possibility of abrupt shocks: instead of smooth upward temperature rises over the next century, we may see rapid, uneven and extreme rises resulting in major ecosystem disruption (Alley et al. 2003) and social breakdown: ice sheet disintegration, interference with major weather systems, the release of frozen sub-oceanic frozen methane hydrate may cause unexpected shifts. So-called runaway climate change is on the agenda. Even a relatively small temperature rise might create vicious circles that could swiftly disrupt equilibrium systems. There may be thresholds and tipping points beyond which rapid and uncontrollable changes will be unleashed.

So abrupt models of change are part of the scientific climate imaginary. But perhaps even more vividly, apocalyptic framings of climate change have dominated in entertainment, news and fiction. They look ahead to scorching heat; chaotic weather events; critical biodiversity loss; rapidly rising sea levels; catastrophic drought. There are glimpses of what is apparently the very end of the world, or civilization at least. Some focus on the short-term future during which societies violently fall apart under new climate pressures. Some look further ahead to the experiences of a few survivors in a post-apocalyptic wasteland and backwards to the imbecility of our own carbon culture. Others imagine a posthuman Eden, a 'world without us' (Weisman 2007; see also Bellamy and Szeman 2014) when the earth's atmospheric equilibrium is reset at a point that no longer supports human life. Much of this imagery is superficial and populist, particularly the violent end-of-days scenarios. For Buell, mainstream media versions of the apocalypse narrative simply offer a spectacle of destruction for entertainment. '[W]recked, militarized, post-natural environments of social meltdown and perpetual high-tech combat' (Buell 2010: 31) become special effects objects for passive consumption. They mask the deep contradictions in the social experience of climate change and its presence in and challenge to everyday life. All too often they also present authoritarian solutions to the deep social upheavals of rapid climate change (Trexler 2015).

Social scientists and campaigners often criticize the catastrophe narrative, suggesting that it produces apathy, indifference, fatalism or conservatism rather than serious commitment to social and political change. Hulme has argued that rhetorics and images of 'catastrophe and chaos' are likely to scare citizens into panicked responses (2008: 232–3).[6] O'Neill and Nicholson-Cole argue that depictions of climate chaos may attract people's attention but generate only fear and feelings of powerlessness and uncertainty that are ineffective for 'motivating genuine personal engagement' (2009: 355). Ereaut and Segnit (2006), in a survey of UK popular media treatments of climate change for the Institute for Public Policy Research in 2006, found that 'alarmism' was one of two dominant repertoires for responding to climate change. Alarmism uses apocalyptic imagery and 'extreme' shock tactics (2006: 13–14) that, they argue, make the climate problem too big and intractable, undermining the resources of hope and agency that would enable people to make changes in their own lives.

Some of these arguments, including those of O'Neill and Nicholson-Cole, are based on qualitative studies of attitudinal responses to images of climate catastrophe. Rather more seem to read large behavioural claims off from a narrow set of texts and deploy a rather reductive model of culture and decoding. More nuanced cultural and political readings (Buell 2010; Gardiner 2010; Skrimshire 2010a, 2010b; Sargisson 2012; Gardner 2015) instead explore the diversity and potential richness of the apocalyptic imagination. Some even suggest that it may be necessary to engage morally and politically with climate change (Buell 2010). If the main policies framing climate change have made it seem manageable and suggested responses of small changes and modification, perhaps apocalyptics offer an alternative paradigm, helping us to register the gravity and urgency of the climate challenge. On this reading, apocalyptic narratives can offer 'a deepening of the imaginative engagement' with the enormity of its temporal and spatial scales (Skrimshire 2010b: 4). Apocalypse might work, in short, to resist the adaptive framework and call attention to the political and ethical drama of the climate challenge. As Skrimshire (2010a) argues, the logic of the apocalyptic narrative from its Biblical roots to its environmentalist reinvention is not simply the fatalistic vision of a violent end but also a new beginning. Apocalypse might open up the possibility of revelation and a transformed world.

The revelatory possibilities of apocalypse are not straightforward, however, as Skrimshire acknowledges (2010a: 229, 233). Amsler argues that the figure of crisis has often stood as the 'basis for critique' and the 'precondition for radical social change' (2010: 129) in critical theory. But Marxist traditions have also struggled to translate diagnoses of objective structural crisis into felt experience. If Jameson (2005) and Bauman (2000) are right that we are now experiencing an almost complete colonization of social and personal life by capitalist values, there are few spaces of hope and multiple opportunities for conservative narratives animated by a 'politics of fear' (Amsler 2010: 129) to mobilize apocalypse to appeal to desires for 'certainty and safety', resist change and shrug off radical critique (p. 139). Swyngedouw (2010) and Blühdorn (2007) argue that populist framings of climate apocalypse, in the context of weak and technocratic mitigation policies, work to obscure or even refuse the possibility of renewal and change. They become 'millennial' visions of 'apocalypse forever' (or 'forever postponed') that suggest not a real historical intervention or the possibility of choices and contestations, only a depoliticized desire to hold onto the same (Swyngedouw 2010: 219).

So there is nothing 'inherently transformative' about apocalypse thinking (Amsler 2010: 140). But there is nothing inherently conservative or fatalistic about it either. As Skrimshire suggests, asking whether or not apocalypse is an appropriate response to climate narratives is the wrong question (2010a: 237). The question misunderstands the complexity of apocalypse narrative and misses the empirical fact of the matter, which is that apocalyptics have been one of the main ways in which Western cultures have tried to come to terms with climate change (Trexler 2015: 82). For Palmer, apocalypse has become such a 'pervasive cultural habit' that it risks falling into cliché and routine (2014: 159). Apocalypse is irrepressibly circulating out there. But it might also stir up ideas that help us extend, resist and complicate narratives of adaptation (Skrimshire 2010a: 237) and keep ethical and political questions on the agenda.

Green hope after the future

So far in this chapter I have looked at dominant framings of environmental crisis in the early twenty-first century, noting both the increasing internalization of environmental crisis *and* proliferating representations of global warming as crisis and apocalypse. These discourses have rewritten the relationship between present and future in environmental debates. Catastrophe collapses into the present, but at the same time it seems that climate and other environmental crises can be managed so that life will go on in ways that are essentially similar to now. In both cases the future seems radically compromised as a space for green hope. In this section I explore the prospects for an environmental utopianism linked to adaptation and apocalypse that is not dependent on positive depictions of sustainable futures or on narratives of radical structural transformation. I consider responses to climate change in the light of theories of ecological modernization that have endorsed small changes and institutional adjustment in response to environmental problems. I ask whether we can be satisfied with the modest, reformist hope they offer. I also briefly explore whether within these self-consciously realist accommodations of climate change there are glimmerings of a 'new civic environmentalism' that might suggest wider and more subversive changes (Dobson 2003). I then draw on theoretical ideas from debates about unsustainability and post-politics to argue for the necessity of apocalyptic visions in contemporary fiction as spaces for imagining how things may go on after the end, between or around crisis and catastrophe.

I go on to look at how changes in the conditions for exploring and expressing green hope have been negotiated in contemporary speculative fiction. I draw in particular on two recent works of ecocritical analysis and science fiction criticism to consider how science fiction is imagining climate change and the Anthropocene. I focus on two authors who are widely seen as among the most committed to keeping alive utopian possibilities in green science fiction: Kim Stanley Robinson, whose eco-utopian novel *Pacific Edge* (1994) we encountered in chapter 4; and Paolo Bacigalupi, whose early twenty-first-century novels *The Windup Girl* (2010) and *The Water Knife* (2015) have won both critical acclaim and wide popular readerships. I draw on Trexler's overview of Anthropocene fiction (2015) and specifically his reading of Robinson's Science in the Capital trilogy as novels of bureaucratic agency to identify a representation of utopian adaptation. I return to Trexler to extend his account of the possibilities and problems of representing environmental apocalypse, drawing also on Vint (2015) and Otto (2014) to unpick how

Bacigalupi's recent post-carbon world-building re-imagines the future in no future.

Ecological modernization and immanent apocalyptics

Advocates of ecological modernization theory (Huber 2004; Jänicke 2004; Mol et al. 2014) argue that modern institutions are reflexive and capable of internalizing environmental challenges with only modest changes. They endorse a pragmatic response to environmental problems, rejecting the need for major political contestation, ethical debate or social transformation. In the last thirty years or so, they argue, we have seen to a greater or lesser degree[7] a greening of major social institutions: sustainable production, green products; domestic practices; transport infrastructures; technological innovation; and policy-making (Mol et al. 2014). The point now is not to look back to root causes of environmental problems but to focus on moving incrementally towards sustainability. Ecological modernization theorists welcome the end of the language of environmental crisis. They argue that environmentalism has moved on from an early preoccupation with limits and the radical critique of capitalist modernity to adopt a more mature and pragmatic focus (Mol and Jänicke 2009: 17). Ecological modernization looks forward to a better, more secure and sustainable society that will develop via continuities with the present. In his review of actually existing and desirable politics of climate change, Giddens explicitly emphasized the anti-utopian element of this argument. Although 'utopian strands will be involved' in any 'positive model of a low-carbon future', radical green visions are unhelpful and a 'hard-headed' approach is now crucial (2011: 11).

Considered in this way, some developments in the multilateral governance of climate change after Kyoto might be seen as modestly utopian. They were not radical or transformative, but they did offer some prospect of addressing emissions and attending urgently to adaptation in the name of a safer and fairer world. Hulme argues that the mid-2000s saw not only a period of consensus on climate change, but also a period of 'optimism and hope' (2009: 332). It appeared to be the end of equivocation, denial and delay on climate matters and the beginning of a time for action on the part of nation states and individual citizens. Much of this hung on the so-called Bali road map (UNFCCC 2007), an action plan for stringent policies on climate mitigation and adaptation adopted at the Bali Climate Change Conference in 2007. It expressed the need for urgency and cooperation in addressing climate change; leveraged multilateral commitments to measurable emissions cuts (UNFCCC 2007: 3); and produced agreements to step up action on adaptation with a particular focus on the Annex 2 countries supporting the immediate needs of the most vulnerable nations (UNFCCC 2007: 4).

The road map did not commit to any particular outcome, but instead inaugurated a process that could hold open the possibility of a safer and more equitable future. For many, particularly UN elites, it seemed an 'exciting and transformational' climate moment (see, for example, the assessment of UNEP Executive Director Achim Steiner in Steiner 2007). For UN Secretary General Ban Ki-moon, new and more stringent measures on climate mitigation and adaptation were attached to an optimistic and positive 'vision of the future' couched in terms of 'green economics' (Ban 2007). The road map would not only move towards greater climate security but create a new round of clean, sustainable global growth. Renewable energy infrastructures would generate jobs and opportunities, even a more responsible capitalism; developed states would do the lion's share of mitigation and support developing nations with technological and infrastructural solutions, regulation, responsibility and (capitalist) regeneration. In retrospect the Bali road map looks like the high point of ecological modernization's hopes for progressive sustainable development and managing climate change without conflict, political contestation or economic pain – indeed, with the promise of economic renewal.

These policies were decisively framed in economistic terms with the commodification of emissions at their centre (Hulme 2009: 302). In 2007 the IPCC Fourth Assessment Report stated that climate change could be addressed with only moderate costs, likely offset by GDP gains resulting from improvements in health and environmental quality.[8] The UK's Stern Review likewise asserted that 'the benefits of strong and early action [on climate change] far outweigh the economic costs of not acting' (Stern 2007: xv). Climate change here is a 'market failure' or economic externality (Stern 2007: xviii) that must be 'internalized' by calculative rationalities.[9] Carbon markets in the form of the Clean Development Mechanism have been central to post-Kyoto reduction policies. In Europe there is now a well-established cap-and-trade Emissions Trading Scheme.[10] It has been widely criticized: caps are set too high; permits too generously distributed; high-emitting nations can refuse to participate, as the US has. The Kyoto Protocol lets polluters offset emissions by investing in emissions reduction projects in the developing world, leading to accusations of a 'carbon colonialism' whereby industrial economies outsource emissions to poorer countries (Hulme 2009: 302; Dobson 2016). And overall global emissions have continued to rise.[11] Whatever the relative successes and failure of particular schemes, however, post-Kyoto climate governance has been extremely effective in commodifying carbon, extending neoliberal rationales to climate management, endorsing the efficiency of the free market, and putting in place a new infrastructure of regulations and market institutions (Hulme 2009).

We might read this marketization of carbon in terms of moves to remove climate change from the public sphere and remake it not as a political and ethical dilemma but as an object to be managed via efficiency and markets (Hulme 2009: 302). In the mid-2000s, after the 4th IPCC and Stern reports, carbon counting was everywhere. Personal carbon calculators sprang up on the internet; the icon of the carbon footprint circulated through popular media and spaces of consumption. Nothing, perhaps, could be a stronger indicator of the internalization of environmental problems than people counting the emissions of their own food or transport choices. Environmental crisis invited us all to become better and more responsible consumers. Here, the space of green desire narrows to market choices and the body and its extensions: the home, personal mobility. It offers better selves and better lifestyles, not a better society or alternative modes of satisfaction (Soper 2000).

But as Dobson (2003) argues, rhetorics and practices of ecological footprinting can also be read as powerful mobilizers of ecological citizenship. They express the complex spatial dynamics of environmental impacts, capturing a sense of our embeddedness in global eco-social networks precisely as consumers – or car drivers or householders. They enable us to think about the common good by meeting us where we are already situated, suggesting possibilities for social change on climate rooted in the mundane everyday, in material-symbolic exchanges, not in abstract ideals of justice or future visions. Counting carbon, then, may be a way to bring environmental ethics and politics into the private realm, stirring a modest utopianism into the quotidian mix. Carbon Rationing Action Groups take counting into a new mode of practice, bringing people together as citizens *and* consumers to commit to voluntary personal carbon allowances. They support each others' emissions reductions and hold themselves collectively accountable; as Carvalho suggests, challenging the dynamics of consumption and global responsibility from the inside (Carvalho 2007, cited in Hulme 2009: 307).

But if there is utopianism here, it is all but dissolved in mainstream processes, restricted by (and to) a rhetoric of small changes that overvalues incremental actions in the present. On this basis we might read reformist environmental policies and appeals to changes in individual behaviour in terms of what Blühdorn calls the 'politics of unsustainability' (2007; Blühdorn 2014). He argues that we have arrived in a post-ecological era characterized by the absence of critique and real alternatives. Environmental issues and green solutions are constantly 'discussed, dissected, evaluated' (Wilson and Swyngedouw 2015: 2), but all that is being done is the performance or management of unsustainability (Blühdorn 2007). Technocratic reform is not painless modernization but a depoliticization of environmentalism's issues and the dissolution of its radicalism. This is contemporary environmental and climate governance as post-politics: techno-managerialism in a public sphere evacuated of political contestation and commitments to opposing models of human well-being and emancipation (Stengers 2015; Wilson and Swyngedouw 2015).

It is in precisely this context that apocalyptic narratives can keep us alive to the impossibilities of the current environmental and climate situation and contest the closure of affirmative post-politics (Buell 2003, 2010; Skrimshire 2010a). The figure of apocalypse may be invaluable to a utopianism contextualized by discourses of endemic crisis. I have suggested in this chapter that the internalization and banalization of environmental crisis has tended to collapse the future into the present or erode its value as a space for imagining otherwise. Apocalypse thematizes and foregrounds this very problem of no future, and asks us how we can learn to live with it. Apocalypse of course can reduce the dilemma to one of mere survival and opens up the prospect of authoritarian solutions. But as Skrimshire (2010a) argues, apocalypse is revelation as well as violent end; it is about disruption and challenge as well as fatalism and fear. In this sense, apocalyptics can be 'revolutionary', asserting that 'another world is possible' (Skrimshire 2010a: 233). The fantasy of apocalypse can register the hope that 'something might intervene in time to force us to change'; it can be 'a mode of critique, a crying out for change' (Canavan 2014: 13).

The apocalypse that is most likely to serve utopian rather than conservative ends, however, is not so much imminent as 'immanent' (Skrimshire 2010a: 220), imploding slowly, as Buell suggests (2003, 2010), in the present, in our homes and into our lifeworlds. A useful apocalypse is less about the end than it is about the prospect of '*no end*: a narrative of a world in which crisis is unfolding constantly' (Skrimshire 2010b: 9; emphasis in original). Biblical apocalypse was about end times and the revelation of a more than human world. Apocalypse remade in the terms of progress and the Enlightenment has become a secular and linear narrative of human possibility – and human hubris and socially made catastrophe (Skrimshire 2010a: 226). In this context the revelation or truth that apocalypse offers is not about whether or not we survive some notional end times, but how to live with ongoing crisis and maintain a commitment to thinking ethically about alternatives. We need to go further into catastrophe and keep reinventing environmental apocalypse, opening it up to 'more intimately realistic portrayals' of environmental damage (Buell 2010: 30) and narratives that '[d]epict humans' one-way trip through time not as a rush to doom, but as a conscious immersion in uncertainty and rising risk' (2010: 30).

Utopia in Anthropocene fictions

Recent science fiction has not been able to offer much in the way of formal green utopian visions. Trexler's survey of 'Anthropocene fiction' (2015) identifies meditations on climate change in literary fiction, thrillers and science fiction, exploring what happens to questions of truth, place, politics and economics under the pressure of heightened awareness and physical evidence of anthropogenic warming. He finds post-apocalyptic scenarios and plots about scientific hoaxes and political failures; moods of dystopian despair, bitter realism, even utopian satire. But he identifies no formal Anthropocene utopias. There are, Trexler concludes, 'fundamental difficulties...in articulating a just and sustainable future' or imagining a 'green revolution' in climate fiction (Trexler 2011: 1; 2015: 135). Canavan notes that in the midst of images of crumbling future cities and toxic natures, ecological science fiction offers unexpected pleasures and fleeting utopian moments: 'the ecstatic vision of improvisational recombinative urban chaos' or 'the way a sunset, shining splendidly through the smog, glistens off the antifreeze' (2014: 3). But it rarely offers detailed descriptions of green utopian societies.

Marge Piercy's *Body of Glass* (1992) depicts a future dominated by the environmental and economic wasteland against which the Mattapoisettans of her *Woman on the Edge of Time* struggled (Moylan 2003). The free village of Tikva embodies a version of the radically egalitarian, ecocentric and creative ethos of the former novel. Maintaining this good society depends on compromise (the Tikvans sell their innovative digital technologies to a multinational corporation to survive), and is limited by a corrupted and depleted ecosystem. Keeping an alternative even partially alive takes flexibility, cunning, nerve, care and amazing self-defence skills – qualities shared out among the daughter, mother and grandmother who are the novel's protagonists. We might read a further reduction of this small and precarious green utopian place in the second novel of Margaret Atwood's MaddAddam trilogy. In *The Year of the Flood* (2009) Toby, the last surviving member of a green cult, gamely tends her plants and tries to care for a motley collection of surviving humans and other animals after a viral pandemic, first on the rooftop of a building in a ruined city, and later in what remains of a high-end sex club, Scales and Tails. One strategy of green speculative fiction, then, has been to create dystopian or post-apocalyptic future societies and to shrink the imagined space of possible green utopian alternatives into its interstices.

Another strategy has been to map the shrinking of the future into the present temporally rather than spatially – narratively collapsing the causes and effects, threats and potentials, of anthropogenic climate change, for all its unimaginably enormous scope and scale, into an always-unfolding near future. This is Kim Stanley Robinson's approach in the three novels comprising the Science in the Capital trilogy (*Forty Signs of Rain*, 2004; *Fifty Degrees Below*, 2005; *Sixty Days and Counting*, 2007). Luckhurst has described this as 'proleptic realism' (2009: 172). The novels are set five minutes ahead of us in an already mutating present, blurring generic boundaries between realism and utopianism in new ways. They refuse any depiction of better or worse future end states, and instead present emergence and flux, flowing and branching moments of discontinuity and continuity. There is no break between the present and a future utopia or dystopia (Prettyman, cited in Trexler 2015: 154). Instead, utopianism is channelled into an expanded present moment of process, where multiple futures constantly emerge. The inevitable effects of global climate change unfold in contingent ways, incrementally and multiply. They produce new possibilities for passivity and accommodation, but also for action and change.

These possibilities are shown to depend for their realization on the willingness and ability of both individual agents and collective agencies to make change. As we saw in relation to *Pacific Edge* (discussed in chapter 4), Robinson does not deal in moments of dramatic revolution or narrate lives of extraordinary heroes. His novels take us into the heart of quotidian experience and small, ordinary successes and failures: messy family life, screwed-up loners, barely functioning institutions and good-enough politicians. *Forty Signs of Rain* (2004) traces the early stages of an abrupt climate event. Parts of the Californian coast erode into the sea; an Atlantic storm floods Washington. We experience this with Frank, a stubborn, frustrated biostatistician; with the Quibler family – Charlie, a green policy wonk, Anna, a science administrator, and their kids; with a group of Buddhist monks serving as ambassadors from their sinking island to the US government. Much of the novel unfolds in office spaces in the National Science Foundation and in Charlie and Anna's increasingly overflowing home (they acquire numerous house guests over the course of the narrative as floods and storm disrupt lives in Washington and beyond). This attention to the ordinary allows the novel to 'span the diverse modalities' of current climate politics across consumer lifestyles, electoral politics, scientific funding bodies and giant geo-engineering projects (Trexler 2015: 169). Trexler argues, though, that Robinson also does something new in these books. He explores specifically bureaucratic agency – change-making in relation to and through organizations: scientific, political, business (2015: 149). In doing so he offers new ways to think about collective politics, not as radically outside or in opposition to mainstream institutions, but emerging in and from them in ways which might diffuse out into transformative effects.

Trexler suggests that Science in the Capital articulates a kind of 'bureaucratic utopianism' (2015: 146). I would like to characterize it in complementary terms as adaptationist utopianism. Trexler argues that in Robinson's novels the complex, multi-layered, many-headed agencies that often seem to stand in the way of positive responses to climate problems can also be mobilized to generate a networked, collaborative, relational power. These are the very institutions that ecological modernizers argue can reflexively adapt to a new environmental and climate reality. Trexler suggests that they are not only a possible source of hope in a climate-changed era; they are a necessary one. Global warming, as we have seen, relentlessly crosses boundaries. It is a hybrid product of a heterogeneous world. It is dizzying in scope, scale, reach and complexity. It will take a relational, networked, ongoing effort to address. The agency needed to deal with climate change is not heroic, nor does it belong to discrete individuals. It is dispersed and diffuse.[12] Trexler then reads Robinson's characterization of the National Science Foundation (and science as an institution) in the novel as self-reflexive, able to reinvent the scientific ethos of public good in order to serve a climate emergency. This model of change is embodied in the person of Diane Chang, head of the National Science Foundation. Diane works by using power productively to enable bottom-up connections and collaborations: stitching together existing research programmes; mobilizing existing knowledge to quickly adapt to new geoclimatic realities; forcing conversations across epistemological boundaries; crafting legislation. Diane's 'bureaucratic genius' is for the 'boring tasks' of administrative life (Trexler 2015: 159). The remaining two novels in the series show how her patient diplomatic work unfolds into world-changing but provisional plans and programmes to manage abrupt climate change and maintain a liveable world.

Climate crisis is not avoided or healed in Robinson's trilogy. But neither is it presented as total and inevitable. It is multiple and relentless, and at the same time manageable and routine. It forces the novels' protagonists to care and to think and act radically in the hope of a better future, but at the same time there is adaptation and reform. The apocalypse presented here, in Skrimshire's (2010a) terms, is immanent. It implodes in the middle of ordinary lives. It brings the future urgently into the present (Trexler 2015: 116). Robinson, like many climate change novelists, uses the figure of flood to locate global warming risks and threats in a particular place. But as Trexler notes, this is 'flood-as-duration', not 'simple apocalypse' (2015: 103, 105). It does not bring a 'single omniscient revelation' but invites 'careful examination of the social mechanisms of the early Anthropocene' (2015: 105). Scenes showing familiar Washington monuments awash are at the same time lively with people – coping, rescuing, adapting. Seen as immanent apocalypse, the climate chaos in Robinson's novels matches the adaptationist utopianism discussed above with the science fictional element of estrangement, unsettling and disruption. As Trexler notes, it is typical of early twenty-first-century narratives of climate change, which move between realism and speculation, disrupting and remaking both genres. Robinson roots speculation firmly in the present; he expands our sense of realism beyond previously understandable figures of self and society to encompass intimations of the enormity of anthropogenic change. He invests utopian hope in both.

Paolo Bacigalupi's *The Water Knife* (2015) likewise figures a kind of immanent apocalypse. If there is adaptation here, however, it is much darker and more dysfunctional than Robinson's. Part dystopia, part thriller, the novel is set in the southwestern United States and a parched and chaotic near future. In Arizona, chronic, convulsive drought is the new normal. Power over everyday life concentrates in the hands of economic and political elites who control water systems and can establish title over rivers and reservoirs, ruthlessly cutting off struggling exurban communities to divert water to more profitable developments. Here it is capitalism that has adapted, ferociously and pitilessly, to the new politics of water scarcity. But, like Robinson, Bacigalupi engages with the big sweep of this future largely in intimate and domestic settings, in the homes of people living in a world after running water. Journalist Lucy Monroe is introduced in her house designed for survival in the desert, sweeping off her solar panels after a dust storm. Maria Villarosa, a teenage refugee from Texas, lives in a temporary shelter become permanent, strewn with clothes that can be washed only occasionally and peeing into a Clearsac, a watertight bag that can filter out drinkable water. Key scenes take place in the apartment of a privileged executive in an Arizona arcology – a luxury, all-inclusive, self-sufficient housing complex. The water knife of the title, Angel Velasquez, is one of the few characters able to move between multiple intimate spaces. Angel survives this dry conflicted world in part because he is never committed to a home from which to experience everyday immanent crisis.

Vint reads the setting for *The Water Knife* as a 'slow-moving apocalypse of environmental collapse' compared to 'Hollywood visions of sensational and swift destruction' (2015: para. 1). If Bacigalupi's speculations have a realist tone, it is because he uses intimate settings 'to make us *feel* as well as understand the future we are rushing toward' (Vint 2015: para. 5; emphasis in original). One of the strengths of Bacigalupi's fiction, as Otto has argued, is its 'ecotopian strategy' of presenting climate disaster as an unavoidable fate (2014: 182). Detailed, powerful speculative fiction allows us to fully project ourselves into it, cognitively and empathetically. From this imagined position, Otto argues, we can see the 'counterfactual possibilities' emergent in the 'past of the future' – that is, the possibilities that still remain in our own present moment (Žižek, cited in Otto 2014: 182). This utopianism, then, depends upon apocalyptic projections and a willingness to forecast futures that are explicitly about the present.

Utopia haunts Bacigalupi's climate futures in other ways too. As Vint notes, the novel is suffused with memories of better futures now lost or rejected. Maria cynically dismisses the stories her Mexican migrant father used to tell about the better life in the North. But the futures of the characters in Bacigalupi's worlds are far from closed or lost, however. They have often lived through a critical moment in which they become estranged from the commonsense of their own cultures, as Otto argues (2014: 183). This leaves them unresigned, open to the contingency of their present moment and what might come. The openness of their futures is terrifying – but vital. In one key passage,[13] Lucy and Angel dispassionately discuss the way life continues after the future has gone. She says, 'I think the world is big, and we broke it. Now…', she goes on,

> I'm not sure we really know anymore. It would be easier to prepare if we had some kind of map that told us what was going to hit us next, except we waited so long, we're off the map. It makes you wonder if anyone is going to actually survive.

Angel replies: 'People will survive. Someone always survives.' When Lucy says she 'didn't peg [him] for an optimist', Angel responds: 'I didn't say it's going to be pretty. But someone, someone will adapt. […] People are adapting and surviving.' They turn to look at the nearby arcology:

> silhouettes of atriums and perhaps even greenery within. A lush place where everyone could go inside and hide. It might be too harsh to live outside, but indoors life could still be

good. With AC and industrial air filters and 90% water recycling, life could still be good. Even in hell.

Like the critical utopians we met in the green utopias of an earlier phase of environmental concern, these characters look forward to a time past their own. Through choice or circumstance, neither seems likely to see out their own lifetime in the privileged enclave of the arcology. Even here, though, there is hope. The novel offers us a conversation that combines apocalypse, adaptation and utopia, inviting the reader to consider 'the productive tension between what is (im)possible for [its] protagonists, and what is still possible for us' (Otto 2014: 189).

Wicked problems and eternal return

Buell argues very powerfully that in the most literal way, environmental crisis has continued and intensified into the twenty-first century. Old problems are worse, and new challenges raise the stakes. We live with 'apocalypse redux' (Buell 2010: 27) despite, or perhaps even because of, the internalization and normalization of environmental crisis. This new iteration of environmental threat comes with the painful knowledge that the warning of the first wave of environmental concern was not heeded, and that the climate change dynamics we now face can be at best managed, not prevented. 'Visions of the future today' thus 'have less of the terrible novelty or even closure they once had...' (Buell 2010: 29). Green utopia has to work in a changed relationship between past, present and future, between everyday crisis and the end of the world.

In this chapter I have rather crudely posed adaptation and apocalypse as antinomies to draw out a series of tensions and impasses around climate crisis that work around the problem of no future. In this, I extend and perhaps oversimplify the suggestion that concludes Skrimshire's discussion of apocalypse as 'eternal return' (2010a: 237). For Skrimshire, eternal return has a double referent. It captures the constant reinvention of the apocalypse narrative through Western history.

It also suggests that the most valuable way to think about apocalypse is as part of a 'continuing, unfolding and transformed reality of which our current actions are unavoidably a part' (2010a: 237). Skrimshire is also suggesting here, I think, that while the apocalyptic imaginary might prime us to resist normalizing crisis, keeping hope and ethics alive in the present, it is also part of that adaptation (Skrimshire 2010: 237). Amsler (2010) suggests that critics are wont to romanticize and overvalue the figure of crisis as containing a gesture towards the transformative and the capacity to stimulate action in the name of a more liberated, fulfilling and greener future. We might need to allow ourselves to be open, then, to the mundane, small changes and subversions that are also now part of green hope after the future.

The challenges of climate change and repeated waves of environmental crisis discourse tend to erase the future as a space for imagining detailed green alternatives to contemporary unsustainable capitalism. We have seen how this is reflected in speculative fiction. Fictive descriptions of ecotopian societies have not entirely disappeared, but they are much scaled down and their power is less evident. But we have also seen that ecotopianism remains very much an important element of some recent Anthropocene speculative fiction. These narratives are reworking old genre boundaries to accommodate a new climate reality. They introduce immanent apocalyptics into depictions of an extended or proleptic present to disrupt climate change denial, indifference and fatalism. At the same time, they imagine ways in which individual and institutional adaption to entirely novel climate challenges might be transformative as well as simply necessary.

After twenty-five years of increasingly urgent reports from the Intergovernmental Panel on Climate Change and global policy since Kyoto, emissions keep rising and no major change is apparent. But as Hulme argues, climate change is not usefully framed as a unitary problem that invites an elegant 'solution' (2009: 333). There can be no singular moment of recognition and revelation, response and implementation. There is just the messy accommodation to a new reality and a new nature (see chapter 6), a revised culture and history. So climate change is a multiple problem framed by diverse, often conflicting, discourses. As Hulme has argued, it is a 'wicked' problem, characterized by complexity and interdependence, cross-cutting different social spheres. It is hard to define, intractable, not amenable to singular and rational solutions or ends. Imagining end states is particularly unhelpful (Hulme 2009: 335). This is why climate change – and, after Buell, the more general problem of environmental crisis redux – makes utopia so difficult. A messy, intractable, open-ended problem which involves the likelihood of real environmental and human damage and loss that are already collapsing into the present does not lend itself to visions of better futures. But this is also why climate change needs utopia, and a processual and open-ended kind of utopianism in particular. Hulme argues that climate change is, in the end, a question. It forces us to ask: What is a good climate? What kinds of human well-being and ecological integrity do we want? What kind of people do we think we are? What kinds of politics can we make? If climate change is a wicked problem, it will need 'clumsy solutions' (Hulme 2009: 337) – complex and even contradictory responses to real-world problems; partial understandings and solutions that will be ad hoc and emergent.[14] The idea of a singular post-carbon utopia, then, is absurd. It is quite possible to think of both mainstream policy solutions and the wildest imaginings of post-apocalyptic dystopian science fiction as contributions to hope in a warming world.

6

After Nature: Ecological Utopianism from Limits to Loss

From no future to no nature

In chapter 5 I explored what happens to green utopianism in cultural conditions of no future. I looked at how green hope is reshaped when environmental crisis ceases to be a future possibility that must – and can – be avoided, and begins instead to seem more like an event that is already unfolding in the present or as inevitable apocalypse. This chapter takes up a different set of concerns prominent in recent ecopolitical philosophy and social theory. It explores arguments about the end of nature and asks what happens to green utopianism if there is no nature to be saved, and if a new relationship with the environment cannot bring about human salvation or a better society. It focuses on arguments that a nature separate from human activities and meanings no longer is, or no longer should be, the privileged object of ecological thought, politics and activism.

These arguments raise important questions for green utopianism. What, if not nature, might inform the content of ecological utopian visions? What could inspire and legitimate environmental utopianism? If nature has ended, does this generate only a sense of loss and pessimism, or can mourning its death produce new forms of utopian hope? Might we even celebrate the end of nature if it frees us from unhelpful attachments to a problematic object? Can we identify new kinds of utopianism in a politics of the real that foregrounds hybrid entities and lively matter? Responses to these questions depend on what we think is at stake in the loss or end of nature. Here I consider two different positions, both of which explore what happens when dominant ideas of nature 'go extinct' (McKibben 2003 [1989]: 48).

The first position links the conceptual death of nature to physical environmental change caused by human activities such that the independence of the nonhuman world loses its meaning. The end of nature is the outcome of empirical changes that can be experienced and measured. The second position frames the end of nature as the loss of a concept, the end of an idea that has also arguably been an ideal. Its proponents claim that we must treat nature as an unhelpful artefact that emerged from modernity's misguided attempts to divide the world into separate spheres: material vs ideal, objective vs subjective (Latour 1991, 2013a). As Thompson points out (2009: 85), the first position frames the end of nature as a matter for regret. It indicates the slipping away of something separate from humans that has for centuries been meaningful and important. Its loss demands an affective response and ethical-political changes. The second position frames the end of the idea of nature as a matter for rejoicing. It indicates the death of an illusion that has prevented us from recognizing the mixed-up human and nonhuman worlds in which we live, and which has stymied the emergence of a truly ecological consciousness, culture and politics.

First, then, I examine claims that nature as a physical reality separate from humans has been destroyed or undermined by human activities. I examine how the spectre of the end of nature has led environmentalists to return to and revise visions of the good green society generated in an earlier phase of environmental politics. I focus on those who have found modest grounds for hope in a sober appraisal of nature's loss, reframing the deep ecological utopian desires that we encountered in chapter 3 via narratives of mourning and grief. I look at McKibben's arguments in *The End of Nature* (2003, first published 1989) and their development both in his own later work (2010) and in the ecological literary criticism of Frederick Buell (2003, 2010). Secondly, I look at arguments from social and political theory that nature is not only not really real, but that it is an obstacle preventing the emergence of a truly environmentalist politics. I focus on Bruno Latour (2004, 2010) and Jane Bennett (2010), both of whom have been widely recognized for their important contributions to novel approaches in ecological politics, philosophy and culture (Wapner 2010; Vogel 2015). They celebrate the end of nature and urge us to live in and with a much richer and more unsettling reality. I position these theorists as articulating a novel kind of utopianism that gestures at the prospects for new forms of collective life.

In the last part of the chapter I explore cultural responses to the idea of the end of nature and the kinds of green utopianism that it might generate. The worlds imagined in recent speculative fiction have spoken both to the new possibilities opened up by proposals for a postnatural and even posthuman metaphysics, and to the sense of loss that the idea of the end of nature generates. As we saw in chapter 4, utopian writers inspired by the ethos of deep ecology made depictions of beautiful wild landscapes an important part of their imagined futures. In these novels, green places, described in detail and with elaborate attention to local particularity, were both objects of political and narrative concern and the material reality in and for which humans act. Those green utopian fictions presented social and economic structures designed for sustainability, but also created cultures in which individuals can fully appreciate the aesthetic and intrinsic value of natural landscapes, thereby adding to their happiness and well-being. In the fictions I consider in this chapter, those landscapes are lost, broken and destroyed, or presented as alien and fantastical. In speculative film especially, landscapes are presented as spectacular, even hyperreal, images, and juxtaposed against narratives of their imminent loss. Contemporary ecological science fiction presents darker futures than those we have previously looked at. But there is the possibility of green hope here too – in mourning the loss of nature; in the celebration of the transformative possibilities of hybrid worlds.

Chapter 5 considered how climate change has been reshaping environmental discourse and politics, in particular via discourses of adaptation which colonize the future, and apocalypse narratives which threaten to erase it. The internalization of environmental crisis has arguably been crucial to main-streaming green issues in Western economies and governance. But it has been accompanied by some broadly conservative and depoliticizing tendencies. Crisis is normalized; the poli-tics of (un)sustainability and ecological modernization domi-nate; responses to climate threats can emphasize holding on to what we have rather than imagining something better. We have seen that green utopianism continues through and within this shift. It is part of the package of adaptive policies and part of the transformative politics of recent climate fic-tions; it can work through narratives of immanent apocalypse to unsettle and resist the status quo. But this green utopianism is perhaps less radical than its deep green predecessors. It is less about nature and more about humans. It is less about collective hope and more about individual choices. It is less about inspiring visions and more about subtly transformative hybrid agencies.

This chapter is also in part about green utopias in a warming era. Claims that we are living through the end of nature are closely related to contemporary understandings of anthropogenic climate change and the cultural reflections of the Anthropocene (Crutzen and Stoermer 2000; Oreskes 2004; Chakrabarty 2009). Indeed, one of the earliest texts to try and make political and cultural sense of the then-emerging science of climate change was also one of the first to suggest an end to nature (McKibben 2003). But 'no nature' responses to climate change differ in important ways from 'no future' ones. No nature arguments seem less conserva-tive. Perhaps perversely – and apparently in tension with the self-professed realism of some of these positions – pronounce-ments about the death of nature can generate radical and even explicitly utopian proposals. McKibben and Buell hope that an affective registering of the loss of nature will generate transformative desires for an overhaul of social, economic and cultural systems. Postnatural theorists are often criticized by environmentalists for being nihilistic or reactionary in invoking postnatural ontologies – but they argue in response that only by rejecting the category of nature can we free up new forms of thought, culture and politics able to resist dualisms and explore new ideas about collective life. The postnatural fictions I examine at the end of the chapter are far from presenting images of a recognizably sustainable or post-carbon society. But they vibrate with an energy and an otherness that might help us to look past 'nature' to a new and more responsible kind of ecologism.

The end of nature, then, does not mean the end of green utopianism. But it does mean mutations and transformations. The content of the green utopia shifts in an era when we are not sure how much nature there is left to save, or whether there ever was any in the first place. In these contexts, environmentalist 'dream[s] of naturalism' (Wapner 2010: 55) look like fantastical projections that protect against the acknowledgement of loss – or are satirized as desperate attempts to hold on to a romantic ideal of aestheticized nature. Deep green visions that root human well-being in empathy with nature lose their grounding. Ecological politics seems stripped of its relatively privileged epistemological and political position as radical and critical. The form of green utopias also changes. Postnatural theorists are explicitly sceptical about the value of speculation and fantasy. But claims about the end of nature can also be a way of holding open the space of the future to the possibility of a different and a better way of living and being.

Mourning the end of nature: loss and hope

Long before Al Gore's inconvenient truth, a prominent American writer and campaigner was articulating an accessible account of climate science, shaping public concern about its implications, and setting the agenda for post-warming environmentalism in contexts not colonized by denial. In 1989 Bill McKibben published *The End of Nature*. Now translated into twenty-four languages, it was lauded as the first mainstream account of climate change and remains a landmark of popular environmental thinking. McKibben's argument combines hard-headed reports on emerging climate science, personal anecdotes, reflections on much-loved landscapes, and engagements with American wilderness writing. But the main message is simple and clear. Human activities are interfering with the nature of nature to the extent that we have 'change[d] the very quality of our relationship with the world around us' (McKibben 2003: 183). Climate change represents the most extreme, irreversible and widespread example of this dynamic:

> By changing the weather we are making every spot on earth man-made and artificial. We have deprived nature of its independence, and that is fatal to its meaning. Nature's independence is its meaning; without it there is nothing but us. (2003: 60–1)

McKibben says he uses the word nature to mean 'a certain set of human ideas about the world and our place in it'. But he is clear also that 'the death of these ideas begins with concrete changes in the reality around us'; changes 'that scientists can measure and enumerate' (McKibben 2003: 7). The idea of wild nature that has nurtured and inspired humans for centuries has survived 'traditional' forms of environmental use and abuse, but 'will not survive the new global pollution' (2003: 60). McKibben is writing, then, about the loss of a physical presence that he believes precedes and exceeds human concerns, activities and meanings. He writes with great feeling about what is slipping away – about America's national parks; Thoreau's wildness (2003: 50–62); the 'buzzing, blooming, mysterious, cruel, lovely globe of mountains, sea, city, forest; of fish and wolf and bug and man; of carbon and hydrogen and nitrogen' (2003: xxv). As human activities grow, nature's vastness, wildness and otherness are reduced and its robust independence becomes needy vulnerability (2003: ix). A particular kind of human being is also lost. McKibben argues that we need 'pristine places' and wild nature (2003: 56, 57) to be fully human. When we are 'no longer part of something larger than ourselves' (2003: 90), we become bigger and stronger – but also less creative, more 'brutish, cloddish' (2003: 91). In the absence of a bigger power (nature, or god; 2003: 82), human lack of self-restraint becomes ugly and destructive.

The rhetoric of *The End of Nature* recalls the 'toxic discourse' that Buell (2001) identifies originating in Carson's *Silent Spring* (1999 [1962]). It speaks of pastoral landscapes tainted by human activities and deploys 'totalizing' imagery of a world with no escape from pollutants (Garrard 2011: 14). Both texts suggest the corruption of a once-pure nature; both invite us to imagine rural America beset by invisible ruin. The memorable opening chapter of Carson's text, 'A fable for tomorrow', sketches a small town in the grip of ecological death; moribund, silent. But Carson's discursive world does have a tomorrow. There is faith in the capacity of nature to endure, and humans to change. By announcing an end that has already taken place, McKibben's 'terminal terminology' (Ronda 2013: para. 3) shifts the register of environmentalist discourse. *The End of Nature* marks a turning point, staging a new 'historical moment' (McKibben 2003: xiv) in which the human relationship with nature has crossed a threshold beyond the point of prevention.

For McKibben, then, we have decisively entered a 'postnatural' era and are living in a new reality (2003: 64). If this state is belied by the apparent persistence of natural beauty in the landscapes around us, it is undeniable when we examine increases in atmospheric greenhouse gases and intensifying warming processes (2003: 65). In these altered times, McKibben argues, future predictions and scenarios are actively unhelpful (2003: 142). Suggesting that we can use the past to predict the future, they reproduce a self-sabotaging belief in the human capacity to foresee and control nonhuman nature. The most basic predictions of rising sea levels bring into play new modes and scales of uncertainty about coastlines, crops, demographics and migration (2003: 117–20). Even the most accurate scenario models merely rehearse the limits of the contemporary imagination in the face of the unimaginable (2003: 143).[1] Life on a warming planet is already happening (2003: 103) – the future is already here, shrinking into the present, speeding up the rate of change in nature (2003: 141). It is already 'too late' to 'reassemble' the natural world (2003: 70, 73). There has been a 'permanent break' (Ronda 2013: para. 3).

In chapter 5 I looked in detail at the temporal dynamics of climate change that McKibben's argument raises in relation to the utopian ideas of the future and environmental crisis narratives. Here I focus on the ontological debates that the end-of-nature proposal dramatizes, that is, the kind of claims it makes about the fundamental constitution of reality, about what exists and the key entities into which our world is divided. Here McKibben's argument in *The End of Nature* can be linked to wider constructionist vs realist debates that were prevalent in the social sciences and humanities when the book was published (Wapner 2010: 16–18). Constructionists in sociology, for example, were arguing that environmental issues are not self-evident realities but rather are only intelligible and understood as problems though active social claims-making (Yearley 1992; Burningham and Cooper 1999; Hannigan 2014) and discursive framings (Hajer 1995, 1996). Humanities scholars were challenging the attachment of US environmentalism to the protection of sacred and separate wilderness, and expressing scepticism that 'nature' could refer to 'One Thing with One Name' (Cronon 1996). Post-structuralists were undermining the ontological categories of nature, culture and humanity, suggesting rather that understanding the world in this way is a product of modernist discourse (Haraway 1991; Latour 1991). Against these various constructionisms, self-identified realists pushed back, asserting a commonsense belief in material nonhuman reality; the distinctive capacity of empirical science to reveal objective truths about the physical world; and a deep ecological commitment to the reality and intrinsic value of nonhuman nature (see, for example, Benton 1994; Martell 1994; Soulé and Lease 1995; Dickens 1996).

McKibben's position is problematic from both sides (Thompson 2009; Vogel 2011). His assertion that nature is unambiguously real and empirically knowable is incompatible with a constructionist position. His insistence that nature is objectively ending is absurd from a realist point of view – quite evidently, nonhuman material processes go on entirely unaffected by McKibben's anguished cry. And his unreconstructed attachment to a romantic ideal of wild nature is uncomfortable for both. Vogel (2011: 85) has shown how, for McKibben's argument to work, nature must be defined as excluding humanity *per se* – in which case anything we do is unnatural and climate change can represent only a quantitative expansion of human effects on the environment, not a qualitative shift across a notional threshold. If humans, however, are always already part of nature, McKibben's position is untenable. Vogel shows how McKibben's argument is rooted in a 'self-defeating' Cartesian binary that ends up producing a kind of inverted anthropocentrism in which human uniqueness always and only ever means a negative capacity to put nature in 'metaphysical peril' (Vogel 2011: 95).[2]

But if *The End of Nature* does not make a rigorous contribution to ontological debates, it is discursively significant in framing and narrating the new conceptual, moral and affective dimensions of environmental dilemmas at the turn of the twenty-first century. It articulates what it feels like to live in and with 'the cumulative, and still accumulating, environmental impact of capitalist development' (Ronda 2013: para. 5). Ronda (2013) argues that McKibben's argument remains powerful not simply because it anticipated growing evidence of physical losses and changes (although it did), but because it provided rhetorical tropes for exploring a new era of loss and environmental uncertainty. These are currently being reasserted and elaborated under the sign of the Anthropocene. Here I understand the Anthropocene both as a (contested) historical epoch defined by the human capacity to alter geological processes, and as a cultural moment marked by repeated and anxious return to the dilemmas that this capacity raises. Like the Anthropocene, the death of nature does not function best as a factual periodization but as a gesture towards the enormity of the ecological transition that we are going through and the gigantic scaling up of collective human agency that it implies (Chakrabarty 2009).

McKibben's thesis, then, can be read as influential articulation of a historically novel feeling of loss in the late twentieth century. It speaks to a lack at the centre of lived experience in relation to what we used to call nature, one that has not been previously articulated in environmentalist discourse. The first wave of post-war environmentalism was framed in terms of limits and crisis, and the second offered a narrative of positive solutions and hope for a common future, as we saw in chapter 2. The first approach projected losses into the future in order to guard against them in the present. The second approach foregrounded saving existing systems and the adoption of new 'development paths' to a secure and sustainable future. Neither left much room to acknowledge environmental losses that were *already* being experienced. The novelty of end-of-nature arguments is to locate environmental issues in an over-determined present 'where nature's time has already run out' (Ronda 2013). These losses continue and intensify even after policy discourses have claimed to be able to solve ecological problems.

McKibben's end is culturally important even if it is logically problematic. I am concerned here with whether it is also generative. Are there sources of green hope after the death of nature? In the original text, McKibben argued that contemplating nature's loss could help raise environmental consciousness and prompt urgent changes in culture and lifestyle. When he subsequently returned to the topic in *Eaarth* (2010), he made the more limited argument that the best we can hope for is to contain the worst extremes of global warming and learn to adapt to life on a harder, meaner planet. In both, McKibben rejects the 'defiant reflex' (2003: 147) – Promethean 'utopias' of technocentrism, rational management and market fixes (2003: 150) – arguing instead for a politics of collective 'restraint' (2003: xvi): smaller, simpler economies; decentralized societies; communities living in place; ecocentric values (see also McKibben 2010: 110–35). He advocates values of 'steadiness', durability and dependability (2010: 103–4), and explores models of small-scale neighbourliness and local production including farmer's markets and transition towns (2010: 110–35).

McKibben's post-carbon society, then, is essentially a rehearsal of the futures we saw in the deep green visions in chapter 4.[3] But McKibben's case for a post-carbon, post-industrial, steady-state society lacks the grounding in nature that framed earlier iterations. If we have already lost nature, how can we save it? McKibben is aware that his position is contradictory; that he urges us to create a future that he says has already been lost (2003: 229). He hopes for 'a relatively liveable world' (2003: 233–5); a world 'less bad than it will otherwise be' (2003: xviii). But he insists we must embrace a grim realism that seems to disallow utopian desire. Indeed, McKibben explicitly rejects the 'what-ifs' and 'we-mights' that framed earlier ecological visions. The metaphor of *Eaarth* is that we have already 'travelled to a new planet, propelled on a burst of carbon dioxide' (McKibben 2010: 45). Earth is no longer the inspiring blue sphere of the first wave of the ecological imagination, but a newly grey and 'inhospitable' place with 'melting poles and dying forests and a heaving, corrosive sea, raked by winds, scorched by heat' (2010: 16, 2). There is no space here for 'fantasies' or 'melodrama' (2010: 100), and no time for 'speculative' or 'imaginative' thinking (2010: xix).[4] We must stoically plan for a 'graceful decline', a 'managed descent' (2010: 99).

But there is nonetheless a utopian charge to McKibben's writing – if not the radical and self-consciously hopeful dreaming of deep ecology, then a muted utopianism of realism and affect. It is linked to what McKibben later called his 'emotional' response to climate change: 'falling in love' with the 'real world' (2005: 182) at the moment of its loss; 'mourning' and sadness for the end; guilt and despair at a world 'mostly us now' (2003: xx). It is also linked to what reads as a visceral distaste for the artificial, 'Astroturf' world (2010: 84) that has now replaced it. Lockwood (2012) shows how, like Carson's *Silent Spring*, McKibben's text uses the revelation of private emotions to mobilize a public issue charged with affect. The idea of the end of nature invites a recognition of the intensity and extent of human re-makings of the world. It shifts the focus of environmentalist discourse away from future threats and promises to dwell instead on an affective registering of loss in the recent past and unfolding present. For McKibben, it is mourning nature's death that may keep alive the desire for a better world, a 'living, eternal, meaningful world' (McKibben 2003: 233).

McKibben's insistence that grief is the only appropriate response to contemporary ecological dilemmas has been read as a weakness. Vogel, for example, suggests that the claim that nature has ended can '*only* lead to sadness about what has been lost' (2011: 85; my emphasis) and that, 'drenched in nostalgia and regret' (Vogel 2015: 29), *The End of Nature* can only look backwards. But he underestimates, I think, the cultural and affective work of narratives of mourning and their potential to produce a utopian effect. Grief can keep alive something of what has been lost, mark its value, and hold open the possibility that we may return again to a better state of things in the future. McKibben might not confidently describe the content of a new nature utopia, but he locates a renewed source of ecological ethics and hope analogous to Baccolini's (2003, 2006) arguments about the utopian value of mourning in fictional dystopias. Baccolini shows how mourning works not only to enable characters to hold on to the memory of what they have lost, but also to articulate what is missing and what matters. Mourning is not conservative or nostalgic but part of a living relationship with the past and an active way of clarifying the desire for something better than the limited present (Baccolini 2003: 130). Below, I look at the work of the ecocritic Frederick Buell to explore how these currents of mourning and loss are at work in popular culture. Before that, however, we will look at a very different take on the end of nature.

Celebrating the end of nature: new materialisms, new possibilities

> When the most frenetic of the ecologists cry out, quaking: 'Nature is going to die', they do not know how right they are. Thank God, nature is going to die. (Latour 2004: 25)

McKibben invites us to look back and mourn the death of a beautiful, separate nature. More recently, however, as Latour's quote above suggests, some social theorists have begun to look forward to its end with glee and eager anticipation. They argue that contemporary environmental problems are not rooted in the empirical death of nature, but in our cultural difficulties in letting go of a fantasy object (Morton 2010) that blocks the development of a truly ecological understanding. Here I focus on the work of Latour (2004, 2010) and Bennett (2010). Both have been influential voices in the emergence of postnatural perspectives in political philosophy. They are particularly interesting in this context for their explicit rejections of older ecocentric ideals, and for the unsettling utopianism that runs through their writing. Both argue that we need to let go of nature to find appropriate ways of attending to a complex and fully interconnected world, one that includes nonhuman others as agents. Nature cannot be the object of and ground for green hope. It has always been a construction, and has become an increasingly irrelevant and problematic one as environmental issues become larger and more visible.

The end of nature would be the death of modernity's most absurd and dangerous illusion, one that prevents us from recognizing the mixed-up human/nonhuman worlds we inhabit.

These thinkers loosely belong to contemporary movements in philosophy, social theory, political thought, human geography, philosophy and cultural analysis that have been referred to as new materialism (Braun and Whatmore 2010; Coole and Frost 2010; Dolphijn and van der Tuin 2012).[5] Although deeply interested in science and bodies, these perspectives do not call for a return to empiricism or endorse older Marxist materialist traditions. Acknowledging the poststructuralist insistence on linguistic and discursive constructions of reality, new materialism nonetheless wants to bring things and object-worlds back into social thinking. It suggests that we might re-situate ecological radicalism in relation to a new ontology. Reality is composed of hybrid entities and complex more-than-human agencies which cannot be divided into separate domains of nature and culture, objects and subjects. The world we have made and must inhabit is a messy, dynamic assemblage of the natural, the technological and the human. There is no room for the nature that has been crucial to those green visions and ecological discourses that since the late 1970s have appeared to hold out the best hope for alternatives to a destructive and instrumental modernity.

One of the voices that have most vociferously and persuasively rejected nature in ecopolitical thought is Bruno Latour. Latour is a sociologist, anthropologist and philosopher. Across a wide range of projects he has investigated the relations among science, nature and the social (Blok and Jensen 2012; Garforth 2015). More accurately, he has explored how we can dispense with these categories in order to know and live with all parts of our shared world differently, and better. In an influential early work, *We Have Never Been Modern* (1991), Latour examined the deep duplicity of Western modernity. In its theories and philosophies, he says, the modern world has treated nature as a separate sphere to culture. In its practices, however (particularly science, engineering and technology), it wildly mixes up natural, cultural and technological things to create new 'imbroglios' (1991: 3). The supposedly separate nature on which culture works, then, and from which politics, the social sciences and the humanities have set themselves apart, is a fiction. There is not one sphere over here of materiality, essence, causality and truth, and another over there of ideas, action, values and opinion. There is only a single reality of hybrid entities and networked agencies.

In *Politics of Nature* (2004), Latour brought these ideas to bear on environmental politics. He argued that ecological philosophy has got it all wrong. It has rushed to put nature on the political agenda and to speak for it in democratic deliberations. But nature is not, as the modern constitution would have us think, a hard material reality: 'a thing, a domain, a realm, an ontological territory' (Latour 2004: 276). It is only 'a jumble of Greek philosophy, French Cartesianism and American parks' (2004: 11). Environmental crisis, Latour suggests, is precisely what emerges when the modern constitution visibly falls apart. It enables us to recognize the mixed-up 'tangle of objects' that modernity has made, and reveals that nature is a mythical category (2004: 24). Ecocentric philosophies suggest that to save nature we must recognize its intrinsic value separate from human culture. But this merely 'rehashes' the binary politics of the modern constitution, substituting a 'greener, warmer' nature for the 'cold grey' nature of science (2004: 18). Latour urges environmentalism to stop clinging to nature. A real political ecology needs to do justice to a much greater human/nonhuman collective, to hybrid entities and irreducibly complex assemblages (2010). We need new conceptual institutions that would enable humans to live a better life in common with multiple others.

The political philosopher Jane Bennett also explores post-natural ontologies and their political implications. In *Vibrant Matter* (2010) she considers the perceptual states, thought-forms and textual processes through which we might attend better to the liveliness of material things. Like Latour, Bennett treats modernity as a mode of thinking that has illegitimately separated vital (human) subjects from dull and inert matter. She uses the notion of vitality to rethink that divide, drawing on philosophical traditions from Spinoza to Bergson to suggest that the world is more like a single dynamic field. '[E]verything is made of the same quirky stuff' (2010: xi) where 'various and variable materialities collide, congeal, morph, evolve, and disintegrate' (2010: xi). Things can 'act as quasi-agents or forces with trajectories, propensities, or tendencies of their own' (2010: viii); human agents are irreducibly material and multiple.

Bennett also aims to show 'how analyses of political events might change if we gave the force of things more due' (Bennett 2010: viii). The environmental crisis is about the increasing visibility of nonhuman and hybrid entities in social life (2010: 1). 'The environment' appears as a matter of political concern at exactly the point that it stops acting as a static and singular backdrop to human life (see also Morton 2007). Bennett, then, is suspicious of deep green philosophy's tendency to 'teleological organicism' (2010: 112), the idea that the natural world has its own logic and that left to its own devices it will bend towards what is right and good – and guide human actors in the same direction. She argues that this is politically naïve and ontologically mistaken. The idea of nature disguises the presence of diverse modes of being and acting in the world and in particular the relentless entanglements of human and nonhuman beings. We must learn to recognize instead of nature a more complex and challenging set of vital, emergent, hybrid energies and agencies at work in the world. 'Wiser interventions into... ecology' and 'more materially sustainable modes of production and consumption' will depend on abandoning nature (2010: xi).

Latour and Bennett, then, show how a new materialism breaks fundamentally with modernist ontologies and characterizes ecocentrism as its equally problematic mirror image. They rule out the possibility of saving or caring for nature as the ground for green hope and thus take a significant turn away from the dominant discourse of post-war environmentalism. Seen from this perspective, as Wapner explains, environmentalism has depended on a 'conceptual boundary' defining wild nature and seeking to protect it from human activities (2010: 41). Separate and pure, nature has embodied many ideas of the good in environmental discourse. It has functioned as 'the beautiful' – an aesthetic ideal, a source of beauty, pleasure and spiritual nourishment (Wapner 2010: 69). It has stood for 'the true', an objective reality or sphere of necessity and authority (2010: 57). And it has modelled 'the right', embodying ethical value and ideas of intrinsic worth beyond the human (2010: 64). In these ways, a 'dream of naturalism' has underpinned green arguments about the good life (Wapner 2010: 55).

After nature, though, the dream of naturalism becomes part of the environmental crisis, not a radical response to it. It functions as an affirmative and escapist ideal of harmony standing in the way of a more effective, engaged environmentalism. For some theorists the problem of naturalism becomes particularly urgent in the light of climate change. Outlining the need for a new politics of global warming, Giddens argues that it will involve 'disavow[ing] any remaining forms of mystical reverence for nature'. The time for ideals of 'living in harmony' with nature or 'respecting the earth' is past. The earth will survive. The challenge is wholly anthropocentric: how do we save existing human societies (Giddens 2011: 56)?

Environmentalism can clearly survive the death of nature and many ecopolitical theorists have embraced the new possibilities that this position presents. Wapner reworks Dobson's light (reformist, anthropocentric) versus dark green (radical, ecocentric) dichotomy to suggest a new 'bright' green environmentalism. It would refuse nature as a meaningful category but embrace wildness and the value of nonhuman others. It would foreground human responsibility for the hybrid assemblages that we have created (2010: 211). Vogel similarly suggests that an environmental ethics without nature would shift away from the desire to conserve and preserve pure wilderness and explore instead how Western societies can take responsibility for the fragmented selves and multiple natures we have created (2011). He suggests that instead of, as Aldo Leopold famously suggested, trying to 'think like a mountain' to see the world from a nonhuman perspective, we would be better off thinking 'like a mall' (Vogel 2015). Vogel shows how ecological thought could start from human artefacts, not nature, especially large, complex objects that have some capacity for self-organization, a teleology, that endure and change over time (Vogel 2015: 155).

With Latour and Bennett, then, theorists like Wapner and Vogel endorse the possibility of an environmental ethics or politics after nature. But I think Latour and Bennett go further to gesture at a distinctive postnatural utopianism. Both are sceptical of conventional utopias. Latour in particular frequently claims that he has 'no utopia to propose' (2004: 163) and is relentlessly critical of modernity's 'dreams of finality and perfection' (2010: 59).[6] Bennett is more open to utopian creativity in green thought as an affirmative supplement to critique (Bennett 2010: 15; see also Braidotti 2013 for a similar argument); and Bennett's work has been convincingly read as utopian by Sargisson (2012). Neither specifies desired ends or offers visions of a greener and more fulfilling society. But they do offer the unsettling and potentially transgressive prospect of thinking and acting without the foundational category of nature. They invite us to recognize new forms of life and lively entanglement between human and nonhuman entities. 'Are you ready,' both ask, 'and at the price of what sacrifice, to live the good life together?' (Latour 1999, cited in Bennett 2010: 109). They register the need and desire for a better way of living in and with our complicated, mixed-up, social, natural and technological worlds. As in the deep ecological philosophy I discussed in chapter 3, the environmental challenge is framed as a metaphysical one (Eckersley 1992): an incitement to re-imagine the world and reinvent the common good.

Bennett and Latour propose new epistemologies and even new institutions for recognizing and managing that common good. Both challenge the taken-for-granted ways in which we understand our world and suggest surprising and estranging alternatives. Latour articulates a boundless optimism for a different and better future in the face of environmental challenges to nature and modernity:

> what risk do we run in trying out a politics without nature? The world is young, the sciences are recent, history has barely begun…and ecology is barely in its infancy: why should we have finished exploring the institutions of public life? (2004: 228)

In *Politics of Nature* (2004), he proposes to show the reader around those institutions rather like the guide in a nineteenth-century utopian novel (Ferns 1999). He translates the ontological questions and debates sketched above into a speculative outline of the postnatural 'successor' (2004: 50) of contemporary politics. He describes this using the metaphor of a bicameral system. The new ecological politics would need two houses. The first or lower house would be responsible for recognizing what kinds of thing matter in the world, for representing the many entities with whom we must live. The second house would have responsibility for overseeing the management of the whole human and nonhuman collective. It would consider how we can live with the new hybrids that our technoscientific society produces. Latour's proposals for new political institutions may not be terribly practical – and they certainly lack the charm, detail and realism of the political institutions imagined and described in formal utopian fiction. But as a provocation to think differently about politics, nature and the organization of our common life, they are challenging and unsettling. They encourage us to explore the 'conceptual institutions' (2004: 42) through which we might more responsibly recognize the common good and to imagine 'self-evidently native forms of life' that do not yet exist (2004: 165).

Bennett's proposal for a successor to modernist binaries focuses less on institutions and more on 'human dispositions, moods and cultural ensembles' (2010: 16). She asks how we might cultivate forms of perception and subjectivity that could attend to the liveliness and 'trenchant materiality' of the nonhuman world (2010: 111). This involves a shift in individual consciousness – a 'newish self' or new kind of 'self-interest' needs to emerge (2010: 113). It also suggests a change in culture or 'regime[s] of perception' (2010: 108). Focusing on simultaneously mundane and awe-inspiring material assemblages, Bennett's text aims to 'experiment with narrating events (encounters with litter, electricity, foods, metal) in ways that present nonhuman materialities as *bona fide* participants rather than as recalcitrant objects, social constructs or instrumentalities' (2010: 62). She focuses on objects and networks that we don't usually associate with nature or environmentalism: electricity, rubbish tips, worms and metal rather than rainforests, trees, polar bears and majestic mountains. She draws us into attenuated encounters with matter by using litanies and lists to convey the quiddity of the phenomenological world, returning again and again to a mundane list of objects ('globe, rat, mat, cap, wood'; 2010: 4). Her writing dwells excessively on moments of perception and affective experience in which things are not settled, whole and final, but instead emerge into a kind of relational indeterminacy that 'shimmer[s]' (2010: 4). Bennett's book, then, as Sargisson (2012) has noted, practises a kind of cognitive estrangement that seems closely related to that of the utopian novels discussed in chapter 4, albeit not in fictional or futuristic terms.

But if this is a mode of utopianism, it differs profoundly from most explicitly utopian theory (Moylan 1986; Jameson 2005; Levitas 2010 [1990]) by rejecting the language of critique. For most theorists, utopia's capacity to generate critical distance from the values, structures and practices of our own society is crucial. Speculation and fantasy, imagining something different, put us at one remove from reality, unsettling its taken-for-grantedness. The new materialists, however, ask us to embrace reality, to describe in detail the social-material worlds we actually live in, not withdraw into the imagination of alternatives. Latour prescribes *more* realism, more 'common sense', as a cure for environmental ills (2004: 8). New materialist theorizing suggests that we need to attend more carefully to the ordinary world under our noses in order to compose a good and liveable community. Although the theoretical context could not be further from McKibben's arguments, the turn away from speculation and appeal to realism is familiar. After nature, then, it seems that green utopianism has to adapt to multiple challenges. The nature that used to ground deep green ethics is gone and some new model of sustainability and the good must be proposed. The loss of that nature must be marked, whether in mourning or celebration. And the relationship between fantasy and reality must be renegotiated. The challenge for Anthropocene utopianism, then, seems to be to find new ways of describing the real world which retain the capacity to unsettle the taken-for-granted and find room for a new, hopeful, recognition of a postnatural common good.

Utopian prospects: nature's absent presence in speculative fiction

I have suggested that in the arguments of both McKibben and the new materialist theorists there is a strand of green utopianism. In McKibben's case this is comparable in content to earlier ecophilosophical visions, albeit more muted and uncertain without the foundation of a separate nature. The green utopian challenge to modernist dualisms in the work of Latour and Bennett is as radical and confident as that earlier generation of ecopolitical philosophers, but rejects the ideal of getting back to nature. In the last section of this chapter, I explore how ideas about the end of nature might be linked to green hope beyond these theoretical accounts, in popular culture and speculative fiction. As we saw in chapter 5, fiction has been exploring the idea of the Anthropocene and the end of a separate nature since McKibben's famous pronouncement. Claims that we live in a postnatural world have not elicited formal, explicit eco-utopian visions. They are more likely to be linked to narratives and images that mourn nature's loss or contemplate its desolation. Some critics argue that elegies for a dead nature can keep alive the hope of a better and more sustainable future. Others suggest that we might find a utopian charge in post-apocalyptic and postnatural scenarios where new possibilities for connections among hybrid objects can be explored. At the same time, idealized landscapes and nature images continue to circulate around popular culture and media, and I consider here whether they may still hold a kind of leftover utopian charge, however limited and debased.

Morton argues that analysts need to look for ecological thinking in literature and film outside the traditions of nature writing and the 'ecomimetic' mode (2007: 31 *et passim*) that were central to an earlier era of literary criticism (Morton 2007; Trexler 2015). Ecomimesis seeks to authentically represent external nature and capture the capacity of sensitive human subjects to respond to it. Far from suggesting new ways of being in the world, Morton argues, it reproduces privileged forms of human subjectivity and reduces nature to landscape. Environmentalist writing has too often celebrated what Morton calls the 'Edenic local' (2010: 51), fetishizing the importance of place-bound perception, satisfied with an aesthetic of limits. Our current postnatural condition demands a new kind of 'ecological thought' that does not depend on the inspiring and consoling figure of a beautiful, separate nature. A truly ecological thought, for Morton, would open up to a bigger, more disturbing and excessive world. It should not offer the beauty of landscape or harmony with nature but instead unsettle us by gesturing at the enormous scale of an interconnected universe and the uncanny experience of living without stable ontological categories.

The ecocentric ideals and Romantic nature aesthetics that Morton describes in terms of the 'Edenic local' have something in common with the green utopias I discussed in chapter 4. When these features appear in contemporary green speculative fiction, it is often in the mode of utopian satire. For example, the first book of Margaret Atwood's MaddAddam trilogy, *Oryx and Crake* (2003), opens with a kind of ironized Eden. We meet a group of innocent, naked creatures, the Crakers. Their needs are simple, their wants are few, and their dispositions are happy. They live simply on grass and roots. We discover via flashbacks that the Craker paradise is not the beginning of a green utopia but rather the outcome of a bio-engineered pandemic, itself the apotheosis of several decades of intensifying climate chaos and social inequality. Nothing is natural here. The Crakers are uncanny nearly-people. They were genetically modified to be peaceful, herbivorous, unreflexive individuals, improvements on the humans who invented them and who have now largely been wiped out in the post-dystopian apocalypse. Their guardian Jimmy, aka the Snowman, can barely exist without the infrastructure of the late twenty-first-century civilization that made him. He survives living in the trees, scavenging food and plastic litter from the beach. The Arcadian utopia and what brought it into being is played for morbid laughs. But the world that modern technoscience and hubris has made is also marked by love and a strange beauty. The Crakers are as often dignified as absurd. It is sometimes a dreamworld as well as a horror show. There are still things worth caring for and saving, as Jimmy does the Crakers.

Trexler (2015) has written about the end of earnest green utopias, reading satires on Edenic harmony as marking the failure of ecocentric aesthetics and ethics of place to do justice to the complexity and scale of climate change. He reads Will Self's (2006) *The Book of Dave* as a grotesque satire on both the dying, dismal, carbon cultures of the late twentieth century and the fantasy that climate catastrophe might 'restore humanity's organic inheritance' (Trexler 2015: 95). It depicts not a 'pastoral utopia' but a primitive future society modelled on the debased values of a late twentieth-century London taxi driver. A violent, misogynist, wilfully ignorant culture sticks closely to the blueprint laid out in the Book, a collection of furious reflections on work and whimsical celebrations of consumption rooted in Dave's experiences behind the wheel of a city cab belching out fumes. The Hamsters of the future certainly live in place and know their local landscape – comprising ruined roads, the remains of factories, genetically modified pigs, and fragments of unbiodegraded plastic which they venerate. The green utopianism of 'perfected nature' (Trexler 2015: 98) is replayed here as a farce of postnatural materialism. Much more relentlessly than in Atwood's novel, the dream of naturalism is buried in bitter laughter.

Some critics suggest that a more useful way of coming to terms with the contemporary environmental predicament is via fictions and films that explicitly figure the death of nature itself and help to articulate an affective cultural response (Buell 2003: 287). As we saw in chapter 5, for Buell the apocalypse predicted by earlier waves of environmentalism is now unfolding in the present and nature has ended. He examines a range of responses to this loss in film, fiction and nature writing, including irony, rage, humour and hyperbole. Most important, he argues, is the capacity of fiction to work in elegiac modes (2003: 303). Mourning makes possible an 'imaginative re-experience [...] of what has been lost' and works against processes of 'habituation and anaesthesia' (Buell 2003: 303). Buell reads late twentieth-century narratives including Joy Williams's novel (2000) *The Quick and the Dead* and Terry Gilliam's film *Twelve Monkeys* (1995) in this frame. Gilliam's film is a science fiction thriller set in various futures. Williams's novel is a broadly realist account of the late twentieth-century present shot through with a vein of heightened speculative fantasy. Both are set in bleak, unstable, degraded environments. Williams's Florida is beset by a 'veritable carnival' of environmental neglect (Buell 2003: 302–3). In the multiple timescapes of *Twelve Monkeys*, environmental collapse has already happened several times over, suggested in a monochrome, claustrophobic underground world of the future and also in the grey, oppressive dead land-scapes of (then) contemporary Baltimore and Philadelphia (2003: 273).

Buell argues that Williams and Gilliam locate the cause of environmental collapse in human cruelty or apathy (2003: 303) and haunt their narrative wastelands with ghosts of a lost nature. Williams's 'wrecked landscapes' are littered with the bones of dead wildlife that 'talk back' (2003: 306), refus-ing the normalization of catastrophe. In *Twelve Monkeys*, nature flickers in bittersweet images on black-and-white tvs, or intrudes as matter out of place as wild animals range through future ruins. Clearly these are not ecotopian visions. But for Buell both speak 'from within crisis-in-progress', refusing to look away from loss, articulating a resistance to environmental decline even if that means mobilizing a 'blind, instinctive, yearning nostalgia' for a nature that never existed (2003: 272). Buell seems to suggest that in times when a positive ecological vision seems impossible, mourn-ing and love can keep open the utopian desire for a better, greener future. But he also treats the death of nature as an empirical fact and suggests that a love of nature is hard-wired into humans in a way that would be problematic for all but the most determined of evolutionary psychologists. And his approach ends in the same impasse that characterizes the contradictions of McKibben's argument: if nature is real and it is dead, then the game is over. Why bother to mourn, let alone hope?

For some theorists, Buell's suggestion that elegy is the appropriate response to the end of nature is both formally problematic and ontologically suspect. It privileges a shortcut to the affective and literary recuperation of what has been lost, assuming that sadness is somehow restorative and that nature continues to matter in its absence. As Ronda notes (2013), the poetic form of the elegy is not easily applied to a supposedly dead nature. In the elegy, the grieving subject is restored to the world by the force of nature itself. This restoration loses its power if nature is gone, if the essence or substance is shattered (Wapner 2010: 166), if we have lost 'the very ground beneath our feet', the very idea of the real (Morton 2010: 31). Like Buell, Morton suggests that we need cultural texts that refuse to look away from loss and ruin. But unlike Buell, he does not think that mourning and melancholic resolution are the right outcome. If we are now after nature, ecological thought and culture must embrace a permanent state of displacement, disorientation and depression (2010: 27). We will have to resist affirmative nature visions, including the consolations of mourning. Instead we need to stay with what is broken, abject and negative.

A 'really deep' ecology, Morton suggests, would be 'dark' (2010: 59). In place of 'affirmative' nature ideals, love of nature and ecomimetic visions, we need texts and aesthetic objects that embody a mood of cold depression (2010: 95). If for Buell humans might be saved by an essential love of nature, for Morton we might be able to anticipate a better way of being only if we are able to grasp our relative insignificance and our complicity in creating and then despoiling a separate nature. One proposal for a dark ecology might be the scenes of a strange, broken world in the animated Disney film *WALL-E* (Stanton 2008).*WALL-E* stands for the many late twentieth- and early twenty-first-century speculative texts that imagine nature's ruin on a planetary scale. The animated film depicts a fallen earth as an unending rubbish dump, abandoned by humanity. Screen after screen is full of technological junk and consumer debris, skyscrapers that are crumbling or even melting. This is not a beautiful, wild or pastoral landscape, and it is not green. It is a vista of bleached-out greys and browns, bathed in an eerie ochre light, everything covered in an ashy layer of dust. As Canavan notes, *WALL-E*, set in 2085, figures the contemporary difficulty of 'imagining an equitable and sustainable future history made by human beings' (2014: 15). Instead the film makes a spectacle of a post-apocalyptic, posthuman and postnatural future. But at the same time, WALL-E, the robot left behind to tidy up Earth after the last of the human population has exiled itself to space, figures the utopian possibilities of 'robots [who] are smart enough to love nature more than we do' (Canavan 2014: 3), and who are able to embody and enact an extraordinary tenderness for both humans and nonhumans (Morton 2010: 86).

In the film, it is robots who enable the fantasy of a return to Earth and a return to nature. *WALL-E*, Canavan suggests, 'pushes us unexpectedly in the direction of utopia'. From the midst of ruin, dirt and dystopia, new possibilities suggest that history remains 'still open and unfixed...unmoored' and 'things, after all, might yet be otherwise' (Canavan 2014: 16). For Morton, the value of art and literature in environmental crisis is its capacity to deal with what is shameful, painful, lost (2010: 10). There are 'seeds of future ways of being together' (2010: 134) here, but you have to wade through a lot of shit to get to them. Postnatural approaches seek an 'uglier and messier intimacy' with nature (Ronda 2013) than we might be quite comfortable with; a non-mimetic and non-innocent ecopoetics (Morton 2010). '[G]limmerings of new times' (Morton 2010: 19), however, may emerge in strange places, in the displaced fragments of an ecological catastrophe that has already happened (2010: 17).

Nature, however, refuses to go away in popular culture and media. If the dream of naturalism now looks unstable or problematic in theory and speculative fiction, it nonetheless remains vivid and ubiquitous in the wider world. Idealized natures, particularly in the form of visual images, continue to circulate extensively and intensively at the moment of its supposed end. Beautiful, largely unpeopled nature parks are at the heart of tourist images. Wildlife documentaries proliferate as biodiversity is threatened. CGI-enhanced pastoral landscapes continue to frame popular fantasy films. For many critical theorists, these are utopian spectacles of the worst kind: mythic images outside history, offering a superficial resolution of environmental problems by appealing to consolatory figures of harmonious landscapes (Luke 1997). Baudrillard argued thirty years ago that nature simulations explode across culture as 'prophylaxis' against the recognition that 'the real planet, presumed condemned' has already been 'sacrificed' (1994: 87).[7] Baudrillard directed his scorn then towards Biosphere II, an attempt to re-create in miniature self-sufficient ecosystems under a dome in Arizona; part science project, part tourist spectacle. Bartram and Shobrook (2000) applied a similar logic to the UK tourist attraction the Eden Project in Cornwall, where visually arresting biomes have been constructed in a reclaimed clay pit, housing mini-rainforests and other non-native ecosystems. The Eden Project, they argue, is a simulated eco-tourist experience offering temporary refuge from ecological anxieties in the spectacle of a redemptive nature.

These are usually seen as corrupt nature utopias, functioning as consolation for the death of nature: protection against its acknowledgement, or a refusal to let go what has already been lost. Latour has applied similar criticisms to the 2009 movie *Avatar* (Cameron 2009), seeing in it another iteration of the same old fantasy of a harmonious green world, this time projected onto a 'Pandora planet' (2013b: 145). As an ecological text, *Avatar* is not transgressive or transformative; it is easy to critique for its conservatism; its gender politics; its uncomfortable reiteration of colonial themes (Canavan 2014). Its rudimentary plot follows a young soldier who learns to love an alien ecocentric culture more than the values of his own patriarchal, exploiting society. *Avatar* appears to offers a back-to-the-planet fantasy, displaced onto another planet. Its overt message is a consolatory vision of ecological connection with nature. But Morton suggests that a 'dark[er] ecological truth' is wired technologically, aesthetically and philosophically into the film. Its ecocentric vision is profoundly unnatural, dependent upon vast and subtle technologies of mediation that cannot be spoken within the world of the film (2014: 220). Its lurid animated aesthetic reiterates a 'naturalistic pastoral' but 'on acid' (p. 220), pushing the viewer constantly to acknowledge that being in touch with nature involves strange encounters with uncanny strangers (2014: 220). And finally, Morton argues, the film cannot suppress that the real encounter with ecology is a recognition of the 'end of the world' (2014: 220) – that is, a recognition of the human capacity for (self-)destruction as military violence that threatens Pandora as climate change threatens Earth. *Avatar* then turns out to be a deeply posthuman and very unsettling vision, even as it apparently stands for the dream of naturalism (Morton 2014: 207).

Green utopianism after the end

In this chapter we have encountered the end of nature in two versions. In one, humans have effectively destroyed the physical world. We must grimly build a small, sadder and more modest society to survive the crisis. In the other, this nature was only ever the 'fantasy object' of modern thought (Morton 2010). We are urged to let go of it in order to apprehend a much bigger, more complex and dynamic postnatural world. These two positions are logically incompatible. But as Wapner (2010) argues, both vividly register important aspects of contemporary relationships with the natural world and present us with similar dilemmas. The end of nature asks us to face up to fundamental uncertainties about the human place in a 'more-than-human world' (Wapner 2010: 24). It asks us to let go of nature and with it some of the holistic and affirmative utopian visions of radical ecology. But it creates space to acknowledge multiplicity, complexity and hybridity. Nature loses its privilege as a source of certainty and authority (Latour 2004; Wapner 2010: 129). But green politics and ethics open up to more demanding and rigorous questions about how we might live better with all the beings that matter.

Read through a postnatural frame, the environmental crisis turns out to be very different to the one articulated in the 1970s. It is not about predictions of hitting limits to growth or the need to protect and value nature. It is the moment at which we find out that there is no nature at all. Environmental crisis is not a turning point that invites us to imagine different future alternatives. It is a longer and slower process of registering fundamental changes that have already happened. In this mode, realism is privileged over speculation and imaginative visions. McKibben's realism operates in a no-nonsense, commonsense register. The geophysical effects of climate change are empirically verifiable and already in train; its social and geopolitical consequences are easily anticipated. We must soberly adapt to an indisputably depleted world. For new materialists, realism means facing a world without the comforts of nature. Reality itself turns out to be much richer and more dynamic than we realized, full of shifts and surprises.

So via the postnatural we lose both the nature that underwrote earlier green utopias and the speculative mode characteristic of utopias more generally. There is no object to save, or to save us. We need to look at what is, not imagine alternatives. But in this context green utopianism matters *more*, not less. By squarely looking at the end of nature and asking what has gone and what is coming next, both environmentalist and new materialist traditions open up new forms of radicalism and hope. McKibben's argument shifts environmentalist discourse from tropes of future limits and development paths and introduces a moral and affective focus on how things are in the here and now. This authorizes a return to the radical ecological visions of the 1970s rather than rehearsing the reformist futures of sustainable development. The new materialists offer a 'rigorous and remorseless theoretical radicalism' (Morton 2010: 134) that enables utopian unsettling. Letting go of nature is not an invitation to despair, but a precondition for exploring the common good of a postnatural and posthuman collective.

It is true that these utopian challenges offer little detail of what social arrangements ought to come after nature. The new materialism offers new ways of looking at caps, mats, gloves and sticks, and new 'conceptual' institutions, but not much in the way of concrete ways of life. Postnatural speculative fictions dwell on what has been lost in a mood of mourning or elegy, post-apocalyptic otherness or lurid pastoral fantasy. They offer unsettling hints of the new ontologies and ethics that must succeed both modernity and ecocentric holism but they do not spell out alternatives. But perhaps, as Wapner argues (2010: 201), this is a time for embracing a radically unsettling uncertainty rather than rushing to solutions. If theoretical responses to the end of nature have been clear and certain in their respective mourning and celebration, cultural responses have been ambivalent and uncertain. Nature is simultaneously loved and missed, anxiously represented and radically absent. Postnatural theorists are keen to celebrate the end or at least get on with letting it go. The rest of us aren't so sure. We are hanging on to something we used to call nature; 'still often haunted or inspired' by the dream of naturalism (Wapner 2010: 130).

Mourning and sadness, then, are part of the uncertain condition of ecological awareness in the Anthropocene. This is the new context for green utopianism. Fleeting moments of desire and hope can be identified in texts that mourn nature's ending, in literatures that attest to its never having existed, and in spectacles that assert its continued beauty and significance. This utopianism is not straightforwardly visionary, and not always critical. Sometimes it is escapist or consolatory. Coming to terms ontologically, politically, ethically and culturally with a 'postnature age' is 'no easy matter' (Wapner 2010: 16). But in the aftermath of nature, the figure of nature itself – as a spectacle, a lost object, or a haunting sense of wildness – continues to mediate utopian hope via both the familiar and the strange.

7
Conclusion: Long Live the Green Utopia?

Nature is dead, and a climate-changed future is already happening. This book ends on a muted note for green utopias. It began by looking at powerful statements that Western societies were heading for environmental overshoot and collapse. It showed how, in the shadow of looming crisis, vivid proposals for a greener, fairer and happier society proliferated. Environmental visionaries said that we could stop economic growth, live peacefully and ethically with nature, and enhance human well-being. They thought we could save the world from damage and depletion and liberate ourselves at the same time. Green utopias worked up proposals for radical sustainability in depth and detail and invited readers to imagine what it would feel like to live in them. For a short period in the 1970s and 1980s there was a blossoming of ecocentric utopian critique and creativity. It was shadowed by the prospect of crisis, but it was radical and optimistic. It contested dominant ideologies and proposed fundamental changes to every aspect of life under late capitalist modernity. Some green political theorists were sceptical about the transformative capacities of this green utopianism, but it made a vital contribution to environmental politics, philosophy and culture.

The book ends by examining the normalization of environmental crisis, the challenge of climate change, and the claim that saving nature to save ourselves was a fundamentally mistaken idea. In policy-making and public debate, environmental crisis now appears as something that can be managed by adapting social and political structures or making small changes in consumer lifestyles. At the same time, there is an uncomfortable awareness that the scale and logic of environmental problems far exceed and outpace our willingness to address them. There is a growing sense that discourses of environmental crisis have not produced real change; that the nature that environmentalists wanted to value and preserve has already been lost. But I have suggested that green utopianism persists after nature and in response to the temporal challenges of climate change and the internalization of environmental crisis. In the compromises of adaptation, in the always-inadequate emissions targets that nations set themselves, in apocalyptic visions, nature spectacles and dark ecologies, in gleefully postnatural theories, there are traces of hope for a better life with what we used to call nature. Mainstream green hope today is cautious, modest and reformist; radical green hope is fragmented, fleeting and compromised. But green utopias have not disappeared.

This last assertion depends, of course, on a very open and broad definition of utopia. I take from Ruth Levitas (2010 [1990]: 9) the idea that utopia's distinctive core is 'the expression of desire for a better way of living and being'. I follow her insight that the forms utopias take, the values they express, and the work they do in our culture are enormously variable (and endlessly interesting, both politically and sociologically). Utopia can also be a method (Levitas 2013) or a hermeneutic. It allows me to dig up implicit visions of the good life in political and policy programmes and examine explicit visions in political philosophy and literature (Levitas's 'archaeological' mode). Looking across these different forms allows me to consider how different kinds of green utopias envisage human and environmental flourishing, what kinds of world they respond to and what alternative ways of being they imagine (Levitas's 'ontological' mode). The hopeful but shallow utopianism in popular environmentalism and global policy-making can be compared with radical ecopolitical visions and similarly unsettling postnatural philosophies. Where the former works around modifications of and continuities with business as usual, the latter imagines a break – in culture, politics and modes of subjectivity. Light green utopianism makes change seem possible in the context of everyday life, but risks commodification and compromise. Dark green utopianism promises metaphysical shifts but risks remaining detached from ordinary experience and romanticizing nature. In the creative spaces of speculative fiction, green utopianism can be both estranging and engaging: creating cognitive and critical distance from the unsustainable world and affectively bringing us close to alternative possibilities.

For Levitas (2013), along with other theorists, a minimal and inclusive definition of utopia is analytically necessary but not sufficient to understanding utopia. It does not capture all that utopias can and should be. It allows us to recognize utopia's ubiquity and its processual, unfinished forms of expression; to reject the idea of utopia as blueprint and goal; to acknowledge a multiplicity of visions of something better. But most utopian theorists are committed to the proposal that utopia is at its best when it is also critical and transformative. They see utopia as valuable primarily insofar as it makes a real intervention in politics and culture. A vague desire for things to be otherwise is not enough. We should seek out and support utopianisms that are active, or, as Moylan has argued, transgressive, transformative and totalizing (2016).[1] We need utopias to fundamentally question what is; to work to make alternatives tangible; and to take issue with the ideological closures that stop us from seeing root problems with whole ways of life, not just piecemeal issues or policies.

I have not been so tied to this political and transformative model of utopianism. In this book I have treated progressive, reformist and partial expressions of green hope – particularly in the context of global environmental policy discourse – as relevant to the discussion. I have valued as utopian theoretical gestures towards a new postnatural collective that may be transformative but which are not necessarily transgressive, and which reject outright the notion of totalizing critique. I observe and compare the emergence and circulation of different utopianisms, some of them weak and compensatory, rather than adding to a singular critical and transformative story of environmental utopianism. This sociological desire to observe and interpret a diversity of green utopianisms at work in the world sometimes lacks a political edge. But it presents quite vividly, I think, a case for the irreducible multiplicity of utopian ideas and for the capacity of utopia to expand and keep alive the space for imagining otherwise.

The figuration and reconfiguration of crisis is key to understanding both changes and continuities in environmental concerns and green utopianism. Crisis isn't what it used to be. Environmental apocalypse has changed since the 1970s. But the continuing resonances of those initial predictions of ecological collapse are part of the cultural resources through which we make sense of climate change today. We saw in chapter 2 the value of the catastrophic horizon for stimulating green visions. In chapter 5 I suggested that this projected crisis can no longer do the same cultural work of authorizing explicit utopian visions set in an imagined future. Both normalization and the new temporal dynamics of climate change have changed the conversation and shifted the grounds for green hope. The early green utopians, especially the fiction writers, found enough resources of hope in radical ecopolitical ideas to shape pictures of a positive, hopeful future founded on values and structures utterly different from our own. The climate fiction of the early twenty-first century, however, resists the formal representation of better utopian societies.

In relation to contemporary climate change debates, then, the future is effaced as a space of projected positive alternatives. The future has already happened or inevitably will. This is partly, of course, about the relentless colonization of the future by capitalist and technocentric logics of growth and efficiency; about hardened neoliberal rhetorics about the end of history; and about the apparent exhaustion of alternatives or the sputtering out of twentieth-century liberatory movements. But it is also about the specificity of climate mechanisms and how they reshape both materially and semiotically the way we orient to the future. Climate change violently reminds us that although the future is contingent, it is by no means wholly open. The carbon societies of the Anthropocene have set out paths and thresholds that must now be navigated. This is not a comfortable thought. But it is not the end of hope either. The intrusion of environmental crisis into the present can be read as the erasure of spaces for utopian thinking and engagement – or as an urgent and immanent challenge to keep hope and radical critique alive and kicking back in the here and now.

We have seen that some philosophers and theorists suggest that a discourse of immanent apocalypse is helpful or necessary for facing up to the challenge of global warming and endemic environmental crisis, either as a corrective to narratives of adaptation or as part of those narratives. There have been celebrations of the end of nature in the midst of contemporary environmental challenges. The much contested but apparently unstoppable and unavoidable idea of the Anthropocene is coming to be associated with hope as much as fear (Proctor 2013). I have suggested that utopian desire survives the end of nature and the erasure of the future. So should we, as Thompson (2009) puts it, 'learn to stop worrying and love climate change'? Thompson suggests that the horror linked to global warming comes from a combination of anticipating the likelihood of enormous human suffering, the moral loss of biodiversity and planetary equilibrium, and an awful recognition of human responsibility for causing change on a planetary scale. But that horror is necessary for change. The 'existential angst' we feel over the human responsibility for something like the end of the world is 'entirely appropriate' (2009: 97). It is the beginning of a new structure of feeling appropriate to the enormity of the situation and the possibility of acting ethically within it.

Stengers suggests that only when we accept that we have entered a new postnatural epoch will we be able to find new 'powers of acting, feeling, imagining, and thinking' in a threatening but invigorating hybrid world (2015: 24). Trexler's analysis of Anthropocene fiction suggests that resources for making sense of that change as 'an emotional, aesthetic and living experience' are already emerging (2015: 6). Indeed, he argues that the very idea of the Anthropocene is the moment at which climate change shifts from being a matter of 'prediction, science, evidence, representation and belief' (Trexler 2015: 3) to a matter of cultural transformation. But if global warming is becoming a lived reality, it is also the moment at which a strange new future presses into the present. As Trexler and other critics have argued, narrative engagements with climate change have demanded the creative use of both realist and speculative genres to negotiate between the intimacy of the causes and effects of contemporary crisis and the enormity of its temporal and spatial scales (Trexler 2015: 12–13). Utopia can be part of that mix.

A good Anthropocene might, then, be possible. But a lot of post-crisis hope is problematic from a more conventionally deep ecological or political ecology perspective. It is in some cases simply a re-inscription of aggressive technocentrism (Proctor 2013; for a critique of an earlier version of some of these arguments, see Buell 2003). Proponents of the new postnatural era have perhaps been too keen to urge us to get over 'bemoaning the loss' and 'get on with the joyful task of managing the earth' (Proctor 2013: 87). There is necessarily fear in the Anthropocene as well as hope – and darkness (Morton 2007, 2010), sadness and doubt (McKibben 2010). Loss and fear are an ineradicable part of our new environmental contexts and are already reshaping the kind of hope that is possible. The powerful metaphysical conviction of deep ecological philosophy that environmental crisis could provide the opportunity for an expansion of individual and collective well-being, that limits need not mean only constraint and sacrifice but renewal and emancipation – that is no longer a part of the green utopian story.

Nor will nature go away easily. Celebrations of its end may be good theoretical hygiene in the face of contemporary environmental dilemmas, but they are empirically short-sighted and culturally unhelpful. Ideas and ideals of nature have been a crucial part of green epistemologies, green hope and green desire until very recently. As we have seen, eco-utopianism can survive claims about nature's end, and environmentalism does not need nature as the chief object and ground for environmental concern. But nature does not disappear when theorists explain it away or activists proclaim its death. It remains as expressive reality, absent presence, spectacle; a matter of love and hope. '[Y]earning for the good old days of Eden' is indissolubly mixed up in 'messy hyperrealities' (Proctor 2013: 87) and hybrid naturecultures (Haraway 2003). We are subject to a 'nostalgia' for nature that is nonetheless built on centuries of 'effective mastery' over it (Proctor 2013: 88). The nature we have first damaged and then tried to protect is now capable of threatening every aspect of our 'modes of thinking' and 'ways of living' (Stengers 2015: 20).

As Proctor argues, then, diverse concepts of nature still suffuse the environmental movement and popular environmentalism. This nature now encompasses ideas about wildness, hybridity and a 350-ppm-CO_2 optimal atmosphere (Proctor 2013: 88). But it is still about 'wilderness, national parks and Gaia', still about beautiful pristine landscapes. And they might still do some good. It is right, as the postnaturalists have argued, to reject binaries and the dualistic separation of nature and culture, the material and the social, the objective and the subjective. As Proctor argues, the tendency of modernists and ecologists to 'stop counting at two' is environmentally problematic. But, as he goes on, replacing dualism with monism is equally problematic; we should not 'stop counting at one' either (2013: 91). It is useful to insist philosophically that we exist in a hybrid singular reality in which distinctions between the natural and the cultural do not make sense. But it is imperative also to insist that as everyday humans we do not meaningfully experience the world as one 'massive mix of nature and culture' (Proctor 2013: 91). We live in and with multiple naturecultures (Haraway 2003); we need to trace many stories that need to be patiently narrated, understood and changed (Haraway 1991).

So I don't defend either a nature-loving or a postnaturalist position in this book. I observe that both can generate green hope. I don't endorse either adaptation or apocalypse in the face of coming climate change. I note that both are woven into the cultural and literary fabric through which we will live with it. I have tried to show that whether or not analysts and critics defend particular utopian visions or types of utopia, they exist anyway. I think green utopias happen without this kind of consent and approval. I think green hope springs up in the unlikeliest of places. The lens of utopian studies is a heuristic that can help us to define, magnify and elaborate utopian desires. I have tried to pick out some examples and take time to critically consider and compare them. But green hopes exist outside my judgement: multiple, perplexing, contradictory, impossible, inspiring. They are always already part of the mix of political, practical and cultural responses to a now-established age of environmental crisis. We are not greeting the Anthropocene with only hope, only fear, only apocalypse, only adaptation. If we have learned nothing else about our environmental predicament since the limits to growth, it is that it is huge in physical and conceptual scale, it is diverse in content, and it is thoroughly (as Hulme 2009 puts it) wicked: multi-dimensional and essentially unresolvable. There is no single or elegant solution. There is no one way of imagining a better post-carbon future. There is always hope.

Notes

Chapter 1: Introduction: Utopia, Environment and Nature

1 In the Marxist critical theory in which these ideas and arguments originate, utopias are often described as the negation of a negation – that is, they refuse (negate) the capitalist denial (negation) of the prospect for real human freedom and fulfilment.

Chapter 2: Environmentalism: From Crisis to Hope

1 In the 1960s there had been an earlier surge of environmentalist activism and activity: the publication of Rachel Carson's *Silent Spring* (1962), the launch of the Whole Earth catalogue, the foundation of the Club of Rome, the publication of Paul Ehrlich's (1971) *The Population Bomb* and Garrett Hardin's (1968) 'Tragedy of the commons' are just some examples.

2 The phrase is from Dryzek (1997: 37).

3 Key theorists include Robert Heilbroner, Garret Hardin and William Ophuls. See Eckersley (1992) for a fuller discussion and references.

4 Other environmental writers of this period used the phrases 'steady-state' (Daly 1973; 1992 [1977]) or 'stable-state economy' (Schumacher 1993 [1973]).

5 Schumacher attributes the opposition between mass production and production by the masses to Gandhi (1993 [1973]: 54).

6 The original blueprint was published in *The Ecologist* journal in 1972 (taking up a whole issue). I refer here to the version published in book form the following year. *The Ecologist*'s Blueprint post-dates *Limits to Growth* and refers to it (see *The Ecologist* 1973: 33).

7 The UNEP was founded as a result of the UN Conference on the Human Environment in Stockholm in 1972. It describes its 'mission' as providing leadership and encouraging partnership in 'caring for the environment by inspiring, informing, and enabling nations and peoples to improve their quality of life without compromising that of future generations' (www.unep.org/about/who-we-are/overview).

8 Local Agenda 21 refers to chapter 28 of Agenda 21, entitled 'Local Authorities' Initiatives in Support of Local Agenda 21' (UNCED 1993: 233–4).

Chapter 3: Deep Ecology: Wild Nature, Radical Visions

1 In my treatment of the principles and ethical commitments of deep ecology here, I risk somewhat glossing important philosophical distinctions, most importantly that between biocentrism and ecocentrism. In debates about ecological philosophy, 'biocentrism' refers to the extension of intrinsic value to include not only human beings but all living beings, so each is treated as having the right to life and flourishing (Curry 2011: 76). This tends, however, to retain the individualism of Enlightenment philosophy and consider only distinct living entities. 'Ecocentrism' properly refers to a more inclusive extension of intrinsic value to all of nature, recognizing the importance not only of individual living beings but the value of complex, interconnected systems (Curry 2011: 57). I have tried to use the term 'ecocentrism' throughout as the one most closely linked with utopian ecological ethics, but my usage is not as precise as that found in more rigorous treatments of ecological philosophy.

2 There were some important overlaps. Naess (1973: 198) refers extensively and approvingly to Schumacher, as do Devall and Sessions (1985). In its early stages, deep ecology often referred to the limits discourse – they didn't criticize the fundamental argument that exponential growth was impossible on a finite planet, but they were sceptical of the

technocratic logics discussed in the previous chapter, and raised new criticisms of its anthropocentrism.

3 Naess in particular was very clear that things would have to get very much worse before the necessity and desirability of a radically ecocentric culture could be recognized (Naess 1989: 23–4).

4 Naess felt it necessary in the mid-1980s to distinguish his own particular deep ecological approach, 'Ecosophy T', from the wider category of deep ecology which he had identified.

5 Naess also refers to the lessons about living lightly on the earth that can be drawn from experiences in wild nature. He mentions the Norwegian tradition of withdrawing to cabin living for non-productive leisure and restoration: the *friluftsliv* (loosely, 'open air life'; 1989: 178). This is a site for the 'spontaneous' recognition of connections with other beings (1989: 167). But Naess stops short of proclaiming wilderness itself as vital to ecological consciousness.

6 The history of ecofeminist debates is much more complex than this, of course. Some feminist thinkers have taken the position that there is a distinctive connection between women and nature rooted in reproductive biology, life-giving capacities and sustenance (even 'creativity'), so that 'reclaiming this connection' was vital both to women's liberation and to generating a constructive anti-anthropocentric politics (Cuomo 2002: 7). The rejection of this strand of ecofeminism, as feminist environmental philosophy entered the academic mainstream in the 1980s, has been widely and contentiously discussed (Cuomo 2002; Mallory 2010).

7 In the survivalist iteration of limits, as we saw in chapter 2, the visions were powerfully centralizing and authoritarian.

8 The substantive ideas are often attributed to indigenous cultures (McGinnis 1999: 2); the term is usually attributed to Allen van Newkirk and said to be coined in 1975 (Aberley 1999: 22).

9 The idea of reinhabitation is particularly associated with the poet and environmentalist Gary Snyder (1990, 1995). For an early philosophical critique of the ideas that would go on to be associated with restoration ecology, see Elliott (1997); for a recent discussion of the complexities of this debate, see Hourdequin (2015: 169–94).

10 Compared with Naess, for example, who was cautious about and uncomfortable with the idea of a pure nature that could

be restored. Naess insisted that nature was always already changed by human practice, and that there was no simple or singular way of reading it as moral.

11 Here I refer primarily to *Towards an Ecological Society* (1988) and *The Ecology of Freedom* (1982). *Remaking Society* (1989) is also relevant.

12 Bookchin's critique of some elements of deep ecology was relentless and vociferous in his later writings; see, for example, *Remaking Society* (1989). He took part in a formal debate in 1989 with Dave Foreman of the radical deep ecology activist group Earth First! This debate was published as *Defending the Earth* (Bookchin and Foreman 1991).

Chapter 4: Utopian Fiction: Imagining the Sustainable Society

1 Jameson has written about eco-anarchism in the work of Ursula Le Guin, in particular how bare, cold landscapes can dramatically expose environmental questions (1975). Moylan (1986) attends closely to the strand of environmentalism in the rich braid of emancipatory political ideas that infuse his critical utopias, but he doesn't separate out the ecological dimensions for explicit attention. There has recently been a renewed attention within science fiction studies to ecological science fiction, including Otto (2012), Canavan and Robinson (2014) and Trexler (2015), some of which looks at ecological utopianism, but not with an exclusive or explicit focus.

2 Thompson refers to Abensour (1973) *Les Formes de l'utopie socialiste-communiste*.

3 The others are: Ursula K. Le Guin's *The Dispossessed*; Samuel R. Delaney's *Triton*; and Joanna Russ's *The Female Man*.

4 As Ferns notes, by having Luciente first visit Connie in her own world, Piercy stages a 'utopian intrusion' that immediately unsettles many of the traditional narrative tropes of the utopian novel, in particular the visitor/guide trope (1988: 462).

5 Le Guin reminds us that 'California was not empty when the Anglos came' (1989: 82).

6 The word affirmation here is interesting in relation to the tradition of critical theory through which utopia has often been discussed. The idea of utopia as the negation of a negation has been particularly important (see chapter 1).

Chapter 5: No Future: Green Utopias between Apocalypse and Adaptation

1 The Living Planet Index (LPI) (http://www.livingplanetindex.
   org/home/index) measures global biodiversity based on
   observations of changes in the populations of a range of
   species. The *Living Blue Planet Report* (2015) used LPI data
   to examine the status of marine biodiversity. It found a 49%
   decline in marine species between 1970 and 2012. A special
   issue of *Science* (Sugden et al. 2015) examined deforestation
   and damage to the health of all three categories of the world's
   forests (boreal, tropical and temperate). This was reported in
   terms of unprecedented levels of loss: see, for example, the
   Carbon Brief report (https://www.carbonbrief.org/scientists-
   warn-of-unprecedented-damage-to-forests-across-the-
   world). The online eco-design journal *Inhabitat* reported
   that forests are 'dying': '[i]t's happening now, it's happening
   fast, and it's even happening in forests that have traditionally
   proven resistant to the changes that endanger other forests'
   (http://inhabitat.com/studies-show-all-major-forest-biomes-
   on-earth-are-dying-and-fast/). Reporting on new migration
   patterns 2010–15, particularly from Syria to Mediterranean
   countries, O'Hagan notes how climate-induced environmental stressors, including drought, are intensifying and
   reshaping political conflicts and economic inequality, with
   significant impacts on migration; climate-inflected migration
   patterns are best understood not as an emergency or a crisis
   but as 'the new normal' (O'Hagan 2015).
2 Even if all GHG concentrations had been stabilized at the
   year 2000 level, further warming at around 0.1°C per decade
   would continue for centuries 'due to the timescales associated with climate processes and feedbacks' (IPCC 2007:
   45–6).
3 UN measures to address climate change begin with the
   Framework Convention on Climate Change (UNFCCC),
   negotiated at the Earth Summit in Rio in 1992 and signed
   into force in 1994. The UNFCCC did not bind nations to
   emissions commitments but set out a broad objective that
   signatories should aim to stabilize greenhouse gas concentrations at safe levels. The UNFCCC formed the basis of the
   Kyoto Protocol, the first international agreement committing
   parties to binding emission reduction targets, adopted in
   1997 and entering into force in February 2005. It committed

signatories who had ratified the Protocol to targets in a
first period 2008–12; this included the EU15 countries and
several other industrial nations. The US has never ratified
the Protocol. A second round of targets was set by the Doha
Amendment to the Kyoto Protocol drafted in 2012 (not yet
ratified) for 2013–20. Thus far, Russia and Japan have also
not accepted second-round targets.

4 The SRES scenarios were introduced in 2000 and used in
the IPCC's third and fourth assessment reports (2001, 2007).
They replaced the earlier IS92 GHG emission scenarios
used since 1992 (including in the IPCC's Second Assessment
Report in 1996). They have now been superseded by four
standard Representative Concentration Pathways (RCPs).

5 The A1 family of scenarios emphasizes rapid economic
growth, intensifying global social convergence, falling population levels after a mid-century peak, and rapid technological development; A1 storylines diverge according to different
energy bases from mid-century (fossil-intensive, non-fossil-
intensive, balanced). A2 storylines emphasize global heterogeneity rather than convergence, with both economic and
technological growth fragmented and slower than A1, and
with increasing global population. B1 scenarios emphasize,
like A1, a convergent and more homogeneous global culture,
this time with modest levels of clean economic growth and
increasingly energy-efficient technologies. B2 scenarios
also emphasize increased sustainability but at a local level
with greater global heterogeneity; population continues to
decrease, economic growth is intermediate, technological
change is fragmentary (IPCC 2000).

6 Hulme also reflects on and contextualizes his own criticism
of the apocalyptic climate narrative as part of his argument
for the value of diverse responses to climate change in the
same discussion.

7 The degree is a matter not of evaluation or theoretical commitment but simply a matter of empirical assessment.

8 Costs of stabilizing atmospheric GHGs below dangerous
levels were estimated at between 0.1 and 0.12% loss of
annual average world GDP growth plus around 5–10% net
additional investment (IPCC 2007: 16, 18).

9 Stern put the costs of mitigation at around 1% of GDP
annually (2006–26) versus minimum losses of 5% of GDP
annually and indefinitely to direct and indirect climate
change costs.

10 Tradable permits for emissions are issued, aimed at enabling the market to decide where, how and when GHGs are emitted beneath an agreed cap.

11 The Global Carbon Project (2015) estimates rises at 60% above 1990 levels, the reference year for Kyoto.

12 In this chapter I focus on the adaptation model of utopian process and the rethinking of futurities explored in recent climate fictions. Trexler's analysis draws on contemporary science studies, in particular Latour's actor-network theory and Star and Griesemer on boundary work and boundary objects, to explore posthuman and postnatural agencies in Anthropocene fiction. In this book I look at some of those ideas and issues in chapter 6.

13 All quotes below are from Bacigalupi (2015), transcribed from the audio-book part 2, from 5 hours 57 minutes.

14 Hulme cites Michael Shapiro and adapts his concept of the 'clumsy institution' (Hulme 2009: 337–8).

Chapter 6: After Nature: Ecological Utopianism from Limits to Loss

1 These ideas, reiterated in McKibben's later reflections on the implications of climate change in *Eaarth* (2010), seem to echo Jameson's influential account of the limits of the utopian imagination; located within the totality of contemporary ideology, it cannot imagine anything truly new but only examine the limits of the present (Jameson 2005).

2 In later work, McKibben accepted some aspects of the philosophical critiques of his position in *The End of Nature* (2005: 184). But he maintains a veneration for 'mother nature' (2003: 91) separate from humanity.

3 McKibben refers approvingly to Earth First (2003: 94), and to Devall and Sessions's (2003: 207–8) desire for 'a different world, where roads are torn out to create vast new wildernesses, where most development ceases, and where much of man's [sic] imprint on the earth is slowly erased' (2003: 194).

4 Despite the clearly speculative idea that underpins the whole book: the figure of a second *Eaarth*.

5 This is a very brief and far from comprehensive list. In different disciplinary traditions, affiliated developments are known as object-oriented philosophy, posthumanism and others.

6 I have argued elsewhere (Garforth 2016) that Latour's notion of utopia is extremely limited and that his anti-utopian

utopianism is very similar to recent reflexive critiques in utopian theory. In particular, his rejection of the ways in which Western modernity has colonized the future with linear, rationalizing visions strongly echoes Le Guin's (1989) arguments.

7 Anticipating Latour's arguments in *Politics of Nature* (2004), Baudrillard (1994) suggests that ecologism itself has been part of this sacrifice, reinventing nature as an object of human concern, bringing it into politics and social meaning, and thus abandoning it to virtuality and mediation.

Chapter 7: Conclusion: Long Live the Green Utopia?

1 'The utopian names a triadic process that is transgressive as it breaks with the status quo, totalizing as it analyzes the entire system that produces the status quo, and transformative as it moves social reality toward a horizon that is comprehensively better for all human beings and indeed for nature itself' (Moylan 2016: 1).

References

Aberley, D. (1999) Interpreting bioregionalism: a story from many voices. In: McGinnis, M. (ed.) *Bioregionalism*. London: Routledge, pp. 13–42.

Alexander, R. (2010) *Framing Discourse on the Environment*. London: Routledge.

Alley, R.B., Marotzke, J., Nordhaus, W.D. et al. (2003) Abrupt climate change. *Science* 299: 2005–10.

Amsler, S. (2010) Bringing hope to 'crisis': crisis thinking, ethical action and social change. In: Skrimshire, S. (ed.) *Future Ethics: Climate Change and Apocalyptic Imagination*. London: Bloomsbury, pp. 129–52.

Anderson, B. (2006a) 'Transcending without transcendence': utopianism and an ethos of hope. *Antipode* 38: 691–710.

Anderson, B. (2006b) Becoming and being hopeful: towards a theory of affect. *Environment and Planning D: Society and Space* 24: 733–52.

Andreas, M. and Wagner, F. (eds.) (2012) *Realizing Utopia: Ecovillage Endeavors and Academic Approaches*. RCC Perspectives 8. Munich: Rachel Carson Center.

Atwood, M. (2003) *Oryx and Crake*. London: Bloomsbury.

Atwood, M. (2009) *Year of the Flood*. London: Bloomsbury.

Baccolini, R. (2003) 'A useful knowledge of the present is rooted in the past': memory and historical reconciliation in Ursula Le Guin's *The Telling*. In: Baccolini, R. and Moylan, T. (eds.) *Dark Horizons: Science Fiction and the Dystopian Imagination*. London: Routledge, pp. 113–34.

Baccolini, R. (2006) Finding utopia in dystopia: feminism, memory, nostalgia, and hope. In: Moylan, T. and Baccolini, R. (eds.) *Utopia Method Value: The Use Value of Social Dreaming*. Oxford: Peter Lang, pp. 159–90.

Baccolini, R. and Moylan, T. (eds.) (2003) *Dark Horizons: Science Fiction and the Dystopian Imagination*. London: Routledge.

Bacigalupi, P. (2010) *The Windup Girl*. London: Orbis.

Bacigalupi, P. (2015) *The Water Knife*, narrated by Almarie Guerra. Audible Studios.

Baker, S. (2006) *Sustainable Development*. London: Routledge.

Bammer, A. (1991) *Partial Visions: Feminism and Utopianism in the 1970s*. London: Routledge.

Ban, K.-M. (2007) A new green economics. *Washington Post*, 3 December. Available at: http://www.washingtonpost.com/wp-dyn/content/article/2007/12/02/AR2007120201635.html.

Bardi, U. (2011) *The Limits to Growth Revisited*. New York: Springer.

Barry, J. (1999) *Rethinking Green Politics*. London: Sage.

Bartram, R. and Shobrook, S. (2000) Endless/end-less natures: environmental futures at the fin de millennium. *Annals of the Association of Human Geography* 90 (2): 370–80.

Baudrillard, J. (1994) *The Illusion of the End* (trans. C. Turner). Cambridge: Polity.

Bauman, Z. (2000) *Liquid Modernity*. Cambridge: Polity.

Bauman, Z. (2003) Utopia with no topos. *History of the Human Sciences* 16 (1): 11–25.

Bauman, Z. (2009 [1976]) *Socialism: The Active Utopia*, 2nd edn. London: Routledge.

Bellamy, B. and Szeman, I. (2014) Life after people: science faction and ecological futures. In: Canavan, G. and Robinson, K.S. (eds.) *Green Planets: Ecology and Science Fiction*. Middletown, CT: Wesleyan University Press, pp. 192–205.

Bennett, J. (2010) *Vibrant Matter: A Political Ecology of Things*. Durham, NC: Duke University Press.

Benton, T. (1994) Biology and social theory. In: Benton, T. and Redclift, M. (eds.) *Social Theory and the Environment*. London: Routledge.

Berg, P. (2002) Bioregionalism: an introduction. *Planet Drum Foundation*. Available at: http://www.planetdrum.org/bioregion_bioregionalism_defined.htm#Bioregionalism.

Berg, P. and Dasmann, R. (1977) Reinhabiting California. *The Ecologist* 7 (10): 399–401.

Berlant, L. (2011) *Cruel Optimism*. Durham, NC: Duke University Press.

Blewitt, J. (2014) *Understanding Sustainable Development*, 2nd edn. London: Routledge.

Bloch, E. (1986) *The Principle of Hope*, 2 vols (trans. N. Plaice). Cambridge, MA: MIT Press.

Blok, A. and Jensen, T.E. (2012) *Bruno Latour: Hybrid Thoughts in a Hybrid World*. London: Routledge.

Blühdorn, I. (2007) Sustaining the unsustainable: symbolic politics and the politics of simulation. *Environmental Politics* 16 (2): 251–75.

Blühdorn, I. (2014) Post-ecological governmentality: post-democracy, post-politics and the politics of unsustainability. In: Wilson, J. and Swyngedouw, E. (eds.) *The Post-Political and its Discontents*. Edinburgh: Edinburgh University Press, pp. 146–68.

Bookchin, M. (1982) *The Ecology of Freedom*. Palo Alto, CA: Cheshire Books.

Bookchin, M. (1988) *Towards an Ecological Society*. Montreal: Black Rose Books.

Bookchin, M. (1989) *Remaking Society*. Montreal: Black Rose Books.

Bookchin, M. and Foreman, D. (1991) *Defending the Earth: A Dialogue Between Murray Bookchin and Dave Foreman*. Boston, MA: South End Press.

Booker, M.K. (1994) *Dystopian Literature: A Theory and Research Guide*. Westport, CT: Greenwood.

Boykoff, M.T., Frame, D. and Randalls, S. (2010) Discursive stability meets climate instability: a critical exploration of the concept of 'climate stabilisation'. *Global Environmental Change* 20 (1): 53–64.

Bradley, K. and Hedrén, J. (eds.) (2015) *Green Utopianism: Perspectives, Politics and Micro-Practices*. London: Routledge.

Braidotti, R. (2013) *The Posthuman*. Cambridge: Polity.

Braun, B. and Whatmore, S. (eds.) (2010) *Political Matter: Technoscience, Democracy and Public Life*. Minneapolis, MN: University of Minnesota Press.

Brereton, P. (2015) *Environmental Ethics and Film*. London: Routledge.

Brown, G., Kraftl, P., Pickerill, J. and Upton, C. (2012) Holding the future together: towards a theorisation of the spaces and times of transition. *Environment and Planning A* 44 (7): 1607–23.

Buell, F. (2003) *From Apocalypse to Way of Life: Environmental Crisis in the American Century*. New York: Routledge.

Buell, F. (2010) A short history of environmental apocalypse. In: Skrimshire, S. (ed.) *Future Ethics: Climate Change and Apocalyptic Imagination*. London: Bloomsbury, pp. 13–36.

Buell, L. (2001) *Writing for an Endangered World: Literature, Culture, and Environment in the US and Beyond*. London: Belknap Press.

Burningham, K. and Cooper, G. (1999) Being constructive: social constructionism and the environment. *Sociology* 33 (2): 297–316.

Cameron, J. [dir.] (2009) *Avatar*.

Canavan, G. (2014) Introduction: if this goes on. In: Canavan, G. and Robinson, K.S. (eds.) *Green Planets: Ecology and Science Fiction*. Middletown, CT: Wesleyan University Press, pp. 1–24.

Canavan, G. and Robinson, K.S. (eds.) (2014) *Green Planets: Ecology and Science Fiction*. Middletown, CT: Wesleyan University Press.

Carson, R. (1999 [1962]) *Silent Spring*. London: Penguin.

Chakrabarty, D. (2009) The climate of history: four theses. *Critical Inquiry* 35: 197–222.

Clark, T. (2015) *Ecocriticism on the Edge: The Anthropocene as a Threshold Concept*. London: Bloomsbury.

Clute, J. (2015) Robinson, Kim Stanley. In: Clute, J., Langford, D., Nicholls, P. and Sleight, G. (eds.) *The Encyclopedia of Science Fiction*. London: Gollancz. Available at: http://www.sf-encyclopedia.com/entry/robinson_kim_stanley.

Commoner, B. (1971) *The Closing Circle: Nature, Man and Technology*. New York: Knopf.

Coole, D.H. and Frost, S. (eds.) (2010) *New Materialisms: Ontology, Agency, and Politics*. Durham, NC: Duke University Press.

Cooper, D. (2014) *Everyday Utopias: The Conceptual Life of Promising Spaces*. Durham, NC: Duke University Press.

Cosgrove, D.E. (1988) *Social Formation and Symbolic Landscape*. Madison, WI: University of Wisconsin Press.

Coupe, L. (ed.) (2000) *The Green Studies Reader: from Romanticism to Ecocriticism*. London: Routledge.

Cronon, W. (1996) Introduction: in search of nature. In: Cronon, W. (ed.) *Uncommon Ground: Rethinking the Human Place in Nature*. New York: Norton, pp. 23–68.

Crutzen, P.J. and Stoermer, E.F. (2000) The 'Anthropocene'. *The International Geosphere-Biosphere Programme (IGBP) Global Change Newsletter* 14: 17–18.

Cuomo, C.J. (2002) On ecofeminist philosophy. *Ethics and the Environment* 7 (2): 1–11.

Curry, P. (2011) *Ecological Ethics: An Introduction*, 2nd edn. Cambridge: Polity.

Daly, H. (ed.) (1973) *Towards a Steady-State Economy*. London: Freeman.

Daly, H. (1992 [1977]) *Steady-State Economics*, 2nd edn. London: Earthscan.

Davies, A. and Leonard, L. (eds.) (2012) *Enterprising Communities: Grassroots Sustainability Innovations.* Bingley: Emerald.

De Geus, M. (1999) *Ecological Utopias: Envisioning the Sustainable Society.* Utrecht: International Books.

Devall, B. (1988) *Simple in Means, Rich in Ends: Practicing Deep Ecology.* London: Greenprint.

Devall, B. and Sessions, G. (1985) *Deep Ecology.* Salt Lake City, UT: Peregrine Smith Books.

Dickens, P. (1996) *Reconstructing Nature: Alienation, Emancipation, and the Division of Labour.* London: Routledge.

Dobson, A. (1995) *Green Political Thought*, 2nd edn. London: Routledge.

Dobson, A. (2003) *Citizenship and the Environment.* Oxford: Oxford University Press.

Dobson, A. (2009) 'All I left behind' – the mainstreaming of environmentalism. *Contemporary Political Theory* 8 (3): 317–50.

Dobson, A. (2016) *Environmental Politics: A Very Short Introduction.* Oxford: Oxford University Press.

Dolphijn, R. and van der Tuin, I. (eds.) (2012) *New Materialism: Interviews and Cartographies.* Ann Arbor, MI: Open Humanities Press.

Doyle, J. (2011) *Mediating Climate Change.* London: Routledge.

Dryzek, J.S. (1997) *The Politics of the Earth: Environmental Discourses.* Oxford: Oxford University Press.

Dubos, R.J. and Ward, B. (1972) *Only One Earth: The Care and Maintenance of a Small Planet.* London: Deutsch.

Eckersley, R. (1992) *Environmentalism and Political Theory: Toward an Ecocentric Approach.* New York: SUNY Press.

The Ecologist (1973) *A Blueprint for Survival.* London: Penguin.

Ehrlich, P.K. (1971) *The Population Bomb.* New York: Ballantine Books.

Elliott, J. (2012) *An Introduction to Sustainable Development.* London: Routledge.

Elliott, R. (1997) *Faking Nature: The Ethics of Environmental Restoration.* New York: Routledge.

Ereaut, G. and Segnit, N. (2006) *Warm Words: How Are We Telling the Climate Story and Can We Tell it Better?* London: Institute for Public Policy Research.

Eyerman, R. and Jamison, A. (1991) *Social Movements: A Cognitive Approach.* Cambridge: Polity.

Ferns, C. (1988) Dreams of freedom: ideology and narrative structure in the utopian fictions of Marge Piercy and Ursula K. Le Guin. *English Studies in Canada* 14 (4): 453–66.

Ferns, C. (1999) *Narrating Utopia: Ideology, Gender, Form in Utopian Literature.* Liverpool: Liverpool University Press.

Firth, R. (2012) *Utopian Politics: Citizenship and Practice*. London: Routledge.

Fitting, P. (1998) The concept of utopia in the work of Fredric Jameson. *Utopian Studies* 2 (9): 14–15.

Fox, W. (1990a) *Towards a Transpersonal Ecology: Developing New Foundations for Environmentalism*. Boston, MA: Shambhala.

Fox, W. (1990b) The meanings of 'deep ecology'. *The Trumpeter* 7: 48–50.

Frankel, B. (1987) *The Post-Industrial Utopians*. Cambridge: Polity.

Fremeaux, I. and Jordan, J. (2010) In search of utopia. *New Internationalist* 438. Available at: https://newint.org/features/2010/12/01/real-life-anarchist-communities/.

Gabrys, J. and Yusoff, K. (2011) Arts, sciences and climate change: practices and politics at the threshold. *Science as Culture* 21 (1): 1–24.

Gardiner, M.E. (2001) *Critiques of Everyday Life*. London: Routledge.

Gardiner, S.M. (2010) Saved by disaster? Abrupt climate change, political inertia and the possibility of an intergenerational arms race. In: Skrimshire, S. (ed.) *Future Ethics: Climate Change and Apocalyptic Imagination*. London: Bloomsbury, pp. 83–106.

Gardner, C. (2015) The apocalypse is easy: limitations of our climate change imaginings. *Demos*, 13 September. Available at: http://www.demosproject.net/the-apocalypse-is-easy-limitations-of-our-climate-change-imaginings/.

Garforth, L. (2005) Green utopias: beyond apocalypse, progress, and pastoral. *Utopian Studies* 16 (3): 393–427.

Garforth, L. (2009) No intentions? Utopian theory after the future. *Journal for Cultural Research* 13 (1): 5–27.

Garforth, L. (2015) Latour, Bruno (1947–). In: Wright, J.D. (ed.) *International Encyclopedia of the Social & Behavioral Sciences*. Cambridge, MA: Elsevier, pp. 414–19.

Garforth, L. (2016) Review of *An Inquiry into Modes of Existence: An Anthropology of the Moderns* by Bruno Latour. *Global Discourse* 6 (1–2): 140–3.

Garrard, G. (2011). *Ecocriticism*, 2nd edn. London: Routledge.

Geoghegan, V. (1987) *Utopianism and Marxism*. London: Methuen.

Giddens, A. (2011) *The Politics of Climate Change*, 2nd edn. Cambridge: Polity.

Gilliam, T. [dir.] (1995) *Twelve Monkeys*.

Glasbergen, P. and Blowers, A. (eds.) (1995) *Perspectives on Environmental Problems*. London: Arnold.

Global Carbon Project (GCP) (2015) Carbon budget and trends 2015. Available at: www.globalcarbonproject.org/carbonbudget.

Gray, J. (2008) *Black Mass: Apocalyptic Religion and the Death of Utopia*. London: Penguin.

Hajer, M.A. (1995) *The Politics of Environmental Discourse: Ecological Modernization and the Policy Process*. Oxford: Clarendon Press.

Hajer, M.A. (1996) Ecological modernisation as cultural politics. In: Lash, S., Szerszynski, B. and Wynne, B. (eds.) *Risk, Environment and Modernity: Towards a New Ecology*. London: Sage, pp. 246–68.

Hannigan, J. (2014) *Environmental Sociology: A Social Constructionist Perspective*, 3rd edn. London: Routledge.

Haraway, D.A. (1991) Cyborg manifesto: science, technology, and socialist-feminism in the late twentieth century. In: Haraway, D.A. *Simians, Cyborgs and Women: The Reinvention of Nature*. New York: Routledge, pp. 149–81.

Haraway, D.A. (2003) *The Companion Species Manifesto: Dogs, People, and Significant Otherness*. Chicago, IL: Prickly Paradigm Press.

Hardin, G. (1968) Tragedy of the commons. *Science* 162: 1243–8.

Harvey, D. (2000) *Spaces of Hope*. Edinburgh: Edinburgh University Press.

Heffernan, N. and Wragg, D.A. (2011) *Culture, Environment and Ecopolitics*. Newcastle: Cambridge Scholars Press.

Hochman, J. (1988) *Green Cultural Studies: Nature in Film, Novel and Theory*. Moscow, ID: University of Idaho Press.

Hourdequin, M. (2015) *Environmental Ethics: From Theory to Practice*. London: Bloomsbury.

Huber, J. (2004) *New Technologies and Environmental Innovation*. Cheltenham: Edward Elgar.

Hulme, M. (2008) Governing and adapting to climate: a response to Ian Bailey's Commentary on 'Geographical work at the boundaries of climate change'. *Transactions of the Institute of British Geographers* 33 (3): 424–7.

Hulme, M. (2009) *Why We Disagree About Climate Change: Understanding Controversy, Inaction and Opportunity*. Cambridge: Cambridge University Press.

Imran, S., Alam, K. and Beaumont, N. (2014) Reinterpreting the definition of sustainable development for a more ecocentric reorientation. *Sustainable Development* 22 (2): 134–44.

Intergovernmental Panel on Climate Change (IPCC) (2000) *Emissions Scenarios: Special Report of Working Group III of the Intergovernmental Panel on Climate Change*. Cambridge: Cambridge University Press.

Intergovernmental Panel on Climate Change (IPCC) (2001) *Climate Change 2001: Impacts, Adaptation and Vulnerability. IPCC Third Assessment Report*. Cambridge: Cambridge University Press.

Intergovernmental Panel on Climate Change (IPCC) (2007) Summary for policymakers. In: Metz, B., Davidson, O.R., Bosch, P.R., Dave, R. and Meyer, L.A. (eds.) *Climate Change 2007: Mitigation. Contribution of Working Group III to the Fourth Assessment Report of the Intergovernmental Panel on Climate Change*. Cambridge: Cambridge University Press.

Intergovernmental Panel on Climate Change (IPCC) (2008) *Climate Change 2007: Synthesis Report*. Geneva: IPCC.

Irwin, A. (2001) *Sociology and the Environment*. Cambridge: Polity.

Ivakhiv, A.J. (2013) *Ecologies of the Moving Image: Cinema, Affect, Nature*. Waterloo, ON: Wilfrid Laurier University Press.

Jackson, T. (2009) *Prosperity without Growth: Economics for a Finite Planet*. London: Routledge.

James, E. (1992) Review of *Pacific Edge* by Kim Stanley Robinson. *Foundation* 54: 123–8.

Jameson, F. (1975) World reduction in Le Guin: the emergence of utopian narrative. *Science Fiction Studies* 2 (3): 221–30.

Jameson, F. (2000) Utopianism and anti-utopianism. In: Hardt, M. and Weeks, K. (eds.) *The Jameson Reader*. Oxford: Blackwell, pp. 382–92.

Jameson, F. (2005) *Archaeologies of the Future: the Desire Called Utopia and other Science Fictions*. London: Verso.

Jamison, A. (2001) *The Making of Green Knowledge: Environmental Politics and Cultural Transformation*. Cambridge: Cambridge University Press.

Jamison, A. (2010) Social movements as utopian practice. In: Jacobsen, M.H. and Tester, K. (eds.) *Utopia: Social Theory and the Future*. London: Routledge, pp. 161–80.

Jänicke, M. (2004) Industrial transformation between ecological modernisation and structural change. In: Jacob, K., Binder, M. and Wieczorek, A. (eds.) *Governance for Industrial Transformation. Proceedings of the 2003 Berlin Conference on the Human Dimensions of Global Environmental Change*. Berlin: Environmental Policy Research Centre, pp. 201–7.

Jennings, T.L. (2011) Transcending the adaptation/mitigation climate change science policy debate: unmasking assumptions about adaptation and resilience. *Weather, Climate, and Society* 3 (4): 238–48.

Johns, A. (2012) Feminism and utopianism. In: Claeys, G. (ed.) *The Cambridge Companion to Utopian Literature*. Cambridge: Cambridge University Press, pp. 174–99.

Kambites, C.J. (2014) 'Sustainable development': the 'unsustainable' development of a concept in political discourse. *Sustainable Development* 22 (5): 336–48.

Kraftl, P. (2006) Ecological architecture as performed art: Nant-y-Cwm Steiner School, Pembrokeshire. *Social and Cultural Geography* 7 (6): 927–48.

Kumar, K. (1987) *Utopia and Anti-Utopia in Modern Times*. Oxford: Blackwell.

Latour, B. (1991) *We Have Never Been Modern*. Cambridge, MA: Harvard University Press.

Latour, B. (1999) *Pandora's Hope: Essays on the Reality of Science Studies*. Cambridge, MA: Harvard University Press.

Latour, B. (2004) *Politics of Nature: How to Bring the Sciences into Democracy*. Cambridge, MA: Harvard University Press.

Latour, B. (2010) An attempt at a 'Compositionist Manifesto'. *New Literary History* 41 (3): 471–90.

Latour, B. (2013a) *An Inquiry into Modes of Existence: An Anthropology of the Moderns*. Cambridge, MA: Harvard University Press.

Latour, B. (2013b) Telling friends from foes in the time of the Anthropocene. In: Hamilton, C., Bonneuil, C. and Gemenne, F. (eds.) *Modernity in a New Epoch*. London: Routledge, pp. 145–55.

Lefebvre, H. (1990 [1971]) *Everyday Life in the Modern World*. New Brunswick, NJ: Transaction Books.

Le Guin, U.K. (1975) *The Dispossessed*. St Albans, Herts: Granada Publishing.

Le Guin, U.K. (1986) *Always Coming Home*. London: Victor Gollancz.

Le Guin, U.K. (1989) *Dancing on the Edge of the World: Thoughts on Words, Women, Places*. New York: Grove Press.

Leonard, L. and Barry, J. (eds.) (2009) *The Transition to Sustainable Living and Practice*. Bingley: Emerald.

Levitas, R. (2000) For utopia: the (limits of the) utopian function in late capitalist society. *Critical Review of International and Political Philosophy* 3 (2–3): 25–43.

Levitas, R. (2008) Be realistic: demand the impossible. *New Formations* 65: 78–95.

Levitas, R. (2010 [1990]) *The Concept of Utopia*. Oxford: Peter Lang.

Levitas, R. (2013) *Utopia as Method: The Imaginary Reconstruction of Society*. Basingstoke: Palgrave Macmillan.

Lockwood, A. (2012) The affective legacy of *Silent Spring*. *Environmental Humanities* 1: 123–40.

Luckhurst, R. (2009) The politics of the network: the Science in the Capital trilogy. In: Burling, W.J., Palumbo, D.E. and Sullivan III, C.W. (eds.) *Kim Stanley Robinson Maps the Unimaginable: Critical Essays*. Jefferson, NC: McFarland & Company.

Luke, T.W. (1997) At the end of nature: cyborgs, 'humachines', and environments in postmodernity. *Environment and Planning A* 29 (8): 1367–80.

Mallory, C. (2010) What is ecofeminist political philosophy? Gender, nature and the political. *Environmental Ethics* 32 (3): 305–22.

Martell, L. (1994) *Ecology and Society: An Introduction*. London: Routledge.

McGinnis, M. (1999) A rehearsal to bioregionalism. In: McGinnis, M. (ed.) *Bioregionalism*. London: Routledge, pp. 1–9.

McKibben, B. (2003 [1989]) *The End of Nature: Humanity, Climate Change and the Natural World*. London: Bloomsbury.

McKibben, B. (2005) The emotional core of the end of nature. *Organization and Environment* 18 (2): 182–5.

McKibben, B. (2009) Surviving climate change through mitigation and adaptation. *Conservation Biology* 23 (4): 796.

McKibben, B. (2010) *Eaarth: Making a Life on a Tough New Planet*. New York: St. Martin's Griffin.

McManus, P. (1996) Contested terrains: politics, stories and discourses of sustainability. *Environmental Politics* 5 (1): 48–73.

McNaghten, P. and Urry, J. (1998) *Contested Natures*. London: Sage.

Meadows, D.H., Meadows, D.L., Randers J. and Behrens, W. (1972) *The Limits to Growth: A Report for the Club of Rome's Project on the Predicament of Mankind*. London: Earth Island.

Meadows, D.H., Meadows, D.L. and Randers, J. (1992) *Beyond the Limits: Global Collapse or a Sustainable Future*. London: Earthscan.

Meadows, D.H., Randers, J. and Meadows, D.L. (2004) *Limits to Growth: The 30-Year Update*. White River Junction, VT: Chelsea Green Publishing.

Menegat, R. (2002) Participatory democracy and sustainable development: integrated urban environmental management in Porto Alegre, Brazil. *Environment and Urbanization* 14 (2): 181–206.

Merchant, C. (1982) *Death of Nature: Women, Ecology, and the Scientific Revolution*. San Francisco, CA: Harper.

Merchant, C. (2003) *Reinventing Eden: The Fate of Nature in Western Culture*. New York: Routledge.

Merrick, H. and Tuttle, L. (2015) Feminism. In: Clute, J., Langford, D., Nicholls, P. and Sleight, G. (eds.) *The Encyclopedia of Science Fiction*. London: Gollancz. Available at: http://www.sf-encyclopedia.com/entry/feminism.

Miles, M. (2008) *Urban Utopias: The Built and Social Architectures of Alternative Settlements*. London: Routledge.

Mol, A.P.J. and Jänicke, M. (2009) The origins and theoretical foundations of ecological modernisation theory. In: Mol, A.P.J.,

Sonnenfeld, D.A. and Spaargaren, G. (eds.) *The Ecological Modernisation Reader: Environmental Reform in Theory and Practice*. London: Routledge, pp. 17–29.

Mol, A.P.J., Spaargaren, G. and Sonnenfeld, D.A. (2014) Ecological modernization theory: taking stock, moving forward. In: Lockie, S., Sonnenfeld, D.A. and Fisher, D. (eds.) *Routledge International Handbook of Social and Environmental Change*. London: Routledge, pp. 15–30.

More, T. (1965 [1516]) *Utopia*. London: Penguin.

Morton, T. (2007) *Ecology without Nature: Rethinking Environmental Aesthetics*. Cambridge, MA: Harvard University Press.

Morton, T. (2010) *The Ecological Thought*. Cambridge, MA: Harvard University Press.

Morton, T. (2013) *Hyperobjects: Philosophy and Ecology after the End of the World*. Minneapolis, MN: University of Minnesota Press.

Morton, T. (2014) Pandora's box: *Avatar*, ecology, thought. In: Canavan, G. and Robinson, K.S. (eds.) *Green Planets: Ecology and Science Fiction*. Middletown, CT: Wesleyan University Press, pp. 206–25.

Moylan, T. (1986) *Demand the Impossible: Science Fiction and the Utopian Imagination*. New York: Methuen.

Moylan, T. (2000) *Scraps of the Untainted Sky: Science Fiction, Utopia, Dystopia*. Boulder, CO: Westview Press.

Moylan, T. (2003) 'The moment is here…and it's important': State, agency, and dystopia in Kim Stanley Robinson's *Antarctica* and Ursula K. Le Guin's *The Telling*. In: Baccolini, R. and Moylan, T. (eds.) *Dark Horizons: Science Fiction and the Dystopian Imagination*. London: Routledge, pp. 135–54.

Moylan, T. (2011) 'N-H-N': Kim Stanley Robinson's dialectics of ecology. *Arena Journal* 35/36: 22–44.

Moylan, T. (2016) Utopia's utopian surplus. Paper presented at University Centre Saint-Ignatius Antwerp Interdisciplinary Academic Seminar: 'Utopia Today: The Future as Horizon for Social and Political Action', 23–25 May, University of Antwerp.

Moylan, T. and Baccolini, R. (eds.) (2007) *Utopia Method Vision: The Use Value of Social Dreaming*. Oxford: Peter Lang.

Murphy, P.D. (2000) *Farther Afield in the Study of Nature-Oriented Literature*. Charlottesville, VA: University Press of Virginia.

Naess, A. (1973) The shallow and the deep, long-range ecology movement. *Inquiry* 16: 95–100.

Naess, A. (1989) *Ecology, Community and Lifestyle: Outline of an Ecosophy* (trans. and ed. D. Rothenberg). Cambridge: Cambridge University Press.

O'Hagan, E.M. (2015) Mass migration is no 'crisis': it's the new normal as the climate changes. *The Guardian*, 15 August.

O'Neill, S. and Nicholson-Cole, S. (2009) 'Fear won't do it': promoting positive engagement with climate change through visual and iconic representation. *Science Communication* 30 (3): 355–70.

O'Riordan, T. (1976) *Environmentalism*. London: Pion.

Oreskes, N. (2004) The scientific consensus on climate change. *Science* 306 (5702): 1686.

Orlove, B. (2009) The past, the present and some possible futures of adaptation. In: Adger, W.N., Lorenzoni, I. and O'Brien, K. (eds.) *Adapting to Climate Change: Thresholds, Values, Governance*. Cambridge: Cambridge University Press, pp. 131–63.

Otto, E.C. (2012) *Green Speculations: Science Fiction and Transformative Environmentalism*. Athens, OH: Ohio University Press.

Otto, E.C. (2014) 'The rain feels new': ecotopian strategies in the short fiction of Paolo Bacigalupi. In: Canavan, G. and Robinson, K.S. (eds.) *Green Planets: Ecology and Science Fiction*. Middletown, CT: Wesleyan University Press, pp. 179–91.

Palmer, C. (2014) Ordinary catastrophes: paradoxes and problems in some recent post-apocalypse fiction. In: Canavan, G. and Robinson, K.S. (eds.) *Green Planets: Ecology and Science Fiction*. Middletown, CT: Wesleyan University Press, pp. 158–78.

Parrinder, P. (2000) *Learning from Other Worlds: Estrangement, Cognition, and the Politics of Science Fiction and Utopia*. Liverpool: Liverpool University Press.

Penley, C. (1986) Time travel, primal scene, and the critical dystopia. *Camera Obscura* 5 (3): 66–85.

Pepper, D. (1984) *The Roots of Modern Environmentalism*. London: Routledge.

Pepper, D. (1991) *Communes and the Green Vision: Counterculture, Lifestyle and the New Age*. London: Green Print.

Pepper, D. (2005) Utopianism and environmentalism. *Environmental Politics* 14 (1): 3–22.

Pickerill, J. (2010) Building liveable cities: urban low impact developments as low carbon solutions? In: Bulkeley, H., Castán Broto, V., Hodson, M. and Marvin, S. (eds.) *Cities and Low Carbon Transitions*. London: Taylor and Francis, pp. 178–97.

Pickerill, J. (2012) The built ecovillage: exploring the processes and practices of eco-housing. In: Andreas, M. and Wagner, F. (eds.) *Realizing Utopia: Ecovillage Endeavors and Academic Approaches*. RCC Perspectives 8. Munich: Rachel Carson Center, pp. 99–110.

Piercy, M. (1979 [1976]) *Woman on the Edge of Time*. London: The Women's Press.

Piercy, M. (1992 [1991]) *Body of Glass*. London: Michael Joseph.

Plumwood, V. (1993) *Feminism and the Mastery of Nature*. London: Routledge.

Plumwood, V. (2001) *Environmental Culture: The Ecological Crisis of Reason*. London: Routledge.

Popper, K. (2013 [1945]) *The Open Society and Its Enemies*. Princeton, NJ: Princeton University Press.

Porritt, J. (2011) Must utopia be sustainable? Talk at the Institute for Advanced Studies, Durham University, 8 February.

Proctor, J.D. (2013) Saving nature in the Anthropocene. *Journal of Environmental Studies and Science* 3 (1): 83–92.

Purdy, J. (2015) *After Nature: A Politics for the Anthropocene*. Cambridge, MA: Harvard University Press.

Redclift, M. (1996) *Wasted: Counting the Costs of Global Consumption*. London: Earthscan.

Roberts, I. (2000) Leicester, environment city: learning how to make Local Agenda 21 partnerships and participation deliver. *Environment & Urbanization* 12 (2): 9–26.

Robinson, K.S. (1993 [1988]) *The Gold Coast*. London: HarperCollins.

Robinson, K.S. (1994 [1984]) *The Wild Shore*. London: HarperCollins.

Robinson, K.S. (1995 [1990]) *Pacific Edge*. London: HarperCollins.

Robinson, K.S. (2004) *Forty Signs of Rain*. London: HarperCollins.

Robinson, K.S. (2005) *Fifty Degrees Below*. London: HarperCollins.

Robinson, K.S. (2007) *Sixty Days and Counting*. New York: Bantam Books.

Ronda, M. (2013) Mourning and melancholia in the Anthropocene. *Post45*. Available at: http://post45.research.yale.edu/2013/06/mourning-and-melancholia-in-the-anthropocene/.

Ross, A. (1991) *Strange Weather: Culture, Science and Technology in the Age of Limits*. London: Verso.

Roszak, T. (1979) *Person/Planet: The Creative Disintegration of Industrial Society*. London: Victor Gollancz.

Ruppert, P. (1986) *Reader in a Strange Land: The Activity of Reading Literary Utopias*. Athens, GA: University of Georgia Press.

Rust, S., Monani, S. and Cubitt, S. (2015) *Ecomedia: Key Issues*. London: Routledge.

Sachs, J.D. (2015) *The Age of Sustainable Development*. New York: Columbia University Press.

Sachs, W. (1994) The blue planet: an ambiguous modern icon. *The Ecologist* 24 (5): 170–5.

Sachs, W. (1999) *Planet Dialectics: Explorations in Environment and Development*. London: Zed Books.

Sale, K. (1985) *Dwellers in the Land: The Bioregional Vision*. San Francisco, CA: Sierra Club.

Sargent, L.T. (1994) The three faces of utopianism revisited. *Utopian Studies* 5 (1): 1–37.

Sargisson, L. (1996) *Contemporary Feminist Utopianism*. London: Routledge.

Sargisson, L. (2000) *Green Utopias of Self and Other*. London: Routledge.

Sargisson, L. (2007a) Imperfect utopias: green intentional communities. *Ecopolitics Online Journal* 1 (1): 1–24.

Sargisson, L. (2007b) Strange places: estrangement, utopianism, and intentional communities. *Utopian Studies* 18 (3): 393–424.

Sargisson, L. (2012) *Fool's Gold: Utopianism in the 21st Century*. Basingstoke: Palgrave Macmillan.

Sargisson, L. and Sargent, L.T. (2004) *Living in Utopia: New Zealand's Intentional Communities*. London: Routledge.

Schumacher, E.F. (1993 [1973]) *Small Is Beautiful: A Study of Economics as if People Mattered*. London: Vintage.

Self, W. (2006) *The Book of Dave*. London: Viking.

Simon, J. and Kahn, H. (1984) *The Resourceful Earth: A Response to Global 2000*. Oxford: Blackwell.

Skrimshire, S. (2010a) Eternal return of apocalypse. In: Skrimshire, S. (ed.) *Future Ethics: Climate Change and Apocalyptic Imagination*. London: Bloomsbury, pp. 219–41.

Skrimshire, S. (2010b) Introduction: How should we think about the future? In: Skrimshire, S. (ed.) *Future Ethics: Climate Change and Apocalyptic Imagination*. London: Bloomsbury, pp. 1–12.

Snyder, G. (1990) The place, the region, the commons. In: Snyder, G. *The Practice of the Wild*. New York: North Point Press, pp. 25–47.

Snyder, G. (1995) Reinhabitation. In: Snyder, G. *A Place in Space: Ethics, Aesthetics, and Watersheds*. Washington, DC: Counterpoint, pp. 183–91.

Soper, K. (1995) *What is Nature? Culture, Politics and the Non-Human*. Oxford: Blackwell.

Soper, K. (2000) Other pleasures: the attractions of post-consumerism. *Socialist Register* 36: 115–32.

Soulé, M.E. and Lease, G. (1995) *Reinventing Nature? Responses to Postmodern Deconstruction*. Washington, DC: Island Press.

Spaargaren, G., Mol, A.P.J. and Buttel, F.H. (eds.) (2000) *Environment and Global Modernity*. London: Sage.

Springett, D. and Redclift, M. (2015) Introduction: history and evolution of the concept. In: Redclift, M. and Springett, D. (eds.) *Routledge International Handbook of Sustainable Development*. London: Routledge, pp. 3–38.

Stableford, B.M. (2015) Ecology. In: Clute, J., Langford, D., Nicholls, P. and Sleight, G. (eds.) *The Encyclopedia of Science Fiction.* London: Gollancz. Available at: http://www.sf-encyclopedia.com/entry/ecology.

Stanton, A. [dir.] (2008) *Wall-E.*

Steiner, A. (2007). Every reason for optimism. *The Guardian*, 5 December. Available at: https://www.theguardian.com/environment/2007/dec/05/bali.climatechange.

Stengers, I. (2015) *In Catastrophic Times: Resisting the Coming Barbarism.* London: Open Humanities Press.

Stern, N. (2007) *The Economics of Climate Change: The Stern Review.* Cambridge: Cambridge University Press.

Sugden, A., Fahrenkamp-Uppenbrink, J., Malakoff, D. and Vignieri, S. (2015) Introduction to special issue. Forest health in a changing world. *Science* 349 (6250): 800–1.

Suvin, D. (1979) *Metamorphoses of Science Fiction.* New Haven, CT: Yale University Press.

Suvin, D. (2010) *Defined by a Hollow: Essays on Utopia, Science Fiction and Political Epistemology.* Oxford: Peter Lang.

Swyngedouw, E. (2010) Apocalypse forever? Post-political populism and the spectre of climate change. *Theory, Culture and Society* 27 (2–3): 213–32.

Szerszynski, B., Lash, S. and Wynne, B. (1996) Introduction: ecology, realism and the social sciences. In: Lash, S., Szerszynski, B. and Wynne, B. (eds.) *Risk, Environment and Modernity: Towards a New Ecology.* London: Sage.

Szerszynski, B., Heim, W. and Waterton, C. (eds.) (2004) *Nature Performed: Environment, Culture and Performance.* Oxford: Blackwell.

Taylor, M. (2014) *The Political Ecology of Climate Change Adaptation: Livelihoods, Agrarian Change and the Conflicts of Development.* London: Routledge.

Thompson, A. (2009) Responsibility for the end of nature: or, how I learned to stop worrying and love global warming. *Ethics and the Environment* 14 (1): 79–99.

Thompson, E.P. (1975) *William Morris: Romantic to Revolutionary*, 2nd edn. New York: Pantheon Books.

Thompson, P. (2013) Introduction: the privatization of hope and the crisis of negation. In: Thompson, P. and Žižek, S. (eds.) *The Privatization of Hope: Ernst Bloch and the Future of Utopia.* Durham, NC: Duke University Press, pp. 1–20.

Torgerson, D. (1995) The uncertain quest for sustainable development: public discourse and the politics of environmentalism. In: Fischer, F. and Black, M. (eds.) *Greening Environmental Politics: The Politics of a Sustainable Future.* London: Paul Chapman.

Torgerson, D. (1999) *The Promise of Green Politics: Environmentalism and the Public Sphere.* Durham, NC: Duke University Press.

Trexler, A. (2011) The climate change novel: a faulty simulator of environmental politics. *Policy Innovations,* 7 November. Available at: http://www.policyinnovations.org/ideas/briefings/data/000230.

Trexler, A. (2015) *Anthropocene Fictions: The Novel in a Time of Climate Change.* Charlottesville, VA: University of Virginia Press.

Turner, G.M. (2008) A comparison of *The Limits to Growth* with 30 years of reality. *Global Environmental Change* 18 (3): 397–411.

United Nations (UN) (1992) *United Nations Framework Convention on Climate Change.* Geneva: United Nations. Available at: https://unfccc.int/resource/docs/convkp/conveng.pdf.

United Nations Conference on Environment and Development (UNCED) (1993) *Agenda 21: Programme of Action for Sustainable Development.* New York: United Nations.

United Nations Framework Convention on Climate Change (UNFCCC) (2007) *Report of the Conference of the Parties on its Thirteenth Session, held in Bali from 3 to 15 December 2007. Addendum Part Two: Action taken by the Conference of the Parties At Its Thirteenth Session.* Available at: http://unfccc.int/documentation/decisions/items/3597.php?such=j&volltext=/CP.13#beg).

Urry, J. (2011) *Climate Change and Society.* Cambridge: Polity.

Vint, S. (2015) Excavating a future. *LA Review of Books,* 22 June. Available at: https://lareviewofbooks.org/article/excavating-a-future/#!.

Vogel, S. (2011). Why 'nature' has no place in environmental philosophy. In: Kaebnick, G.E. (ed.) *The Ideal of Nature: Debates about Biotechnology and the Environment.* Baltimore, MD: Johns Hopkins University Press, pp. 84–97.

Vogel, S. (2015) *Thinking Like a Mall: Environmental Philosophy after the End of Nature.* Cambridge, MA: MIT Press.

Wapner, P. (2010) *Living Through the End of Nature: The Future of American Environmentalism.* Cambridge, MA: MIT Press.

Wark, M. (2015) *Molecular Red: Theory for the Anthropocene.* London: Verso.

Warren, K.J. (1996) *Ecological Feminist Philosophies.* Bloomington, IN: Indiana University Press.

Weisman, A. (2007) *The World Without Us.* New York: Picador.

Whittaker, S. (ed.) (1995) *First Steps: Local Agenda 21 in Practice – Municipal Strategies for Sustainability as Presented at Global Forum 94 in Manchester.* London: HMSO.

Williams, J. (2000) *The Quick and the Dead.* New York: Knopf.

Williams, R. (1978) Utopia and science fiction. *Science Fiction Studies* 5 (3): 203–13.

Wilson, J. and Swyngedouw, E. (2015) Seeds of dystopia: post-politics and the return of the political. In: Wilson, J. and Swyngedouw, E. (eds.) *The Post-Political and its Discontents*. Edinburgh: Edinburgh University Press, pp. 1–24.

World Commission on Environment and Development (WCED) (1987) *Our Common Future*. Oxford: Oxford University Press.

WWF (2015) *Living Blue Planet Report: Species, Habitats and Human Well-Being*. Gland, Switzerland: WWF.

Yanarella, E.J. (2001) *The Cross, the Plow and the Skyline: Contemporary Science Fiction and the Ecological Imagination*. Parkland, FL: Universal Publishers.

Yearley, S. (1992) *The Green Case: A Sociology of Environmental Issues, Arguments and Politics*. London: Routledge.

Yearley, S. (1996) *Sociology, Environmentalism and Globalisation*. London: Sage.

Zovanyi, G. (2012) *The No-Growth Imperative: Creating Sustainable Communities under Ecological Limits to Growth*. London: Routledge.

Index